HERBAL BONSAI

D0756742

COLLECTION MANAGEMENT

9/09 07		

57 02788 4

HERBAL BONSAI

Practicing the Art with Fast-Growing Herbs

RICHARD W. BENDER

STACKPOLE
BOOKS

Published by
STACKPOLE BOOKS
5067 Ritter Road
Mechanicsburg, PA 17055

Printed in the United States of America

Cover design by Tina Marie Hill
Illustrations by Becki Bender

Photograph credits:
Richard W. Bender, pp. 8, 11, 29, 30, 74, 75, 77, 81, 83, 84, 96
Scott Elmquist, front cover, pp. 46, 60, 65, 88
Anita Golden, back cover, color section

First edition

10 9 8 7 6 5 4

Library of Congress Cataloging-in-Publication Data

Bender, Richard W.
    Herbal bonsai : practicing the art with fast-growing herbs/
Richard W. Bender. — 1st ed.
        p.   cm.
    Includes bibliographical references.
    ISBN 0-8117-2788-2
    1. Bonsai. 2. Herbs. I. Title.
SB433.5.B44   1996
635.9'772—dc20

95-50604
CIP

635.9772

To the memory of my father, Richard R. Bender

When I was just a lad, he taught me how to grow plants. He encouraged and supported me in growing a large vegetable garden and starting a successful produce stand that sold our harvest in the neighborhood for twenty years. He taught me the value of hard work and set me on the path that supports his grandchildren today. They in turn are learning, working, and earning in our family bonsai business. He has left a legacy that will last for generations.

CONTENTS

PREFACE

THERE ARE THOSE who protest that herbs are an unsuitable subject for true bonsai. A few artists have experimented with rosemary or other herbs, often with some amusement or even a comment like "This is not real bonsai." If you believe bonsai must be hundreds of years old, I hope your grandchildren appreciate it when your potted trees become bonsai. But if a bonsai is an artistic representation in a pot of a magnificent aged tree, then a one-and-a-half-year-old dwarf basil that may not survive another year can be a beautiful bonsai specimen. Don't let the rigid rules of tradition blind your view. Open up to the extended possibilities of bonsai as well as life.

1

History and Change in the Art of Bonsai

BONSAI IS THE art of training a tree to grow on a small scale in a container yet resemble a full-size, aged tree as seen in the wild. The word *bonsai* originally comes from the two Chinese characters *p'en* and *tsai,* meaning a potted tree. The Japanese translated *p'en tsai* to *bonsai,* by which it has become known all over the world.

The first misperception to clear up about bonsai is the pronunciation. There seems to be great confusion about how to pronounce this word. This matters a great deal because of the connotations associated with these different pronunciations and the philosophical underpinnings of the art of bonsai.

Bonsai is commonly mispronounced banzai, like the war cry uttered by kamikaze warriors in Hollywood's B movies as they dive their planes into ships. This is a violent expression of death and destruction, an ending. Properly pronounced, the word is bone-sigh, which can evoke a mystical feeling of hard-soft beauty appropriate to a choice subject of this centuries-old art form: hard because of the gnarled, aged appearance of these trees and the severe treatment—whether by man or nature—required to develop a good bonsai; soft because of the delicate beauty and gracefulness exhibited by the best bonsai specimens.

Unlike static art forms such as a drawing or painting, a bonsai is a living work of art, a live "sculpture" that never stops growing or changing. Such a piece of art is never finished, and old bonsai are often handed down from father to son, with specimens more than 250 years old in existence. This concept dominates the philosophy underlying bonsai. More

1

than just creating an object of beauty, the cultivation of bonsai brings about an understanding of evolution and change, of the growth and development that underscore all of nature. Just as a bonsai is bent and shaped, pruned yet allowed to grow in certain directions, a properly developed human soul undergoes similar transformations. Bonsai is a profound meditative practice that develops discipline and an understanding of life.

This aspect of bonsai is why the art form is so often associated with the philosophical development cultivated by the hard-soft, violent-graceful forms of karate and other martial arts. This association has been most recently seen in the *Karate Kid* series of popular movies. This cultural phenomenon not only increased public awareness of and interest in karate, but has done the same for bonsai as well.

Although just recently increasing in popularity in the United States, bonsai has a tradition thousands of years old. The earliest known examples of a tree growing in a pot come from carved and painted walls in ancient Egyptian tombs dating back about four thousand years. It is not known whether any of these trees were grown for artistic purposes, much less with the concept of growing miniature trees as bonsai. Around 1000 B.C., Hindu doctors in India grew medicinal herbs and trees in pots and tried to keep them dwarfed for ease of transport. These plants were probably pruned to produce the maximum amount of herb rather than for any aesthetic purpose. By early in the first millennium (200 to 400 A.D.), there were a number of established schools or styles of dwarf trees that were associated with different geographical provinces of China.

The first written references to *p'en tsai* come from around 400 A.D., during the Chin dynasty period, by which time bonsai as an art form was well developed. The first paintings of bonsai in evidence are from the Tang dynasty just two hundred years later. These paintings also show widespread use of kiln-fired ceramic pots for bonsai—a thousand years before the Japanese developed such pottery. Pots from this period still exist in museums. By the time of the Sung dynasty around 1000 A.D., much literature was produced about bonsai, including poetry and descriptions of technique. During the later Ming and Ching dynasties, bonsai became very popular among all segments of society, from the rulers and monks to the common people.

It was during the Sung dynasty that bonsai was introduced to Japan, probably by Buddhist monks. The first written and illustrated records of bonsai in Japan come from shortly after 1300 A.D. By the middle of the nineteenth century, bonsai had been developed into its modern form. This art became so pervasive in Japanese culture that most people now associate bonsai with Japan. Of course, Japan did introduce bonsai to the West near the end of the last century—first to Europe and Great Britain, then to the United States. The first real wave of popularity for bonsai in the States came after American GIs were exposed to it during World War II. The biggest surge of interest occurred after the recent series of *Karate Kid* movies, when a whole new generation was exposed to bonsai. What they saw was primarily junipers, leading many to believe that bonsai were a type of miniature juniper. This led to an interest in a few specific types of traditional Japanese bonsai.

Bonsai has had a long tradition in the West as being very difficult or impossible to keep alive. The first bonsai brought to Europe did not do well in the different climate. Many were lost in the first few exhibitions, and this started rumors of mysterious oriental secrets needed to keep them alive. This misperception was magnified with the new popularity of bonsai in the United States after the *Karate Kid* movies. Many people wanted juniper bonsai like they saw in the movie. Unfortunately, most of them wanted to keep the plants indoors, and junipers are difficult to keep alive as houseplants. This is true of most varieties of hardy trees that are used as bonsai subjects.

Traditional varieties such as pine, juniper, maple, elm, and holly grow slowly and need outdoor conditions year-round. They may be brought inside to display, but only for short periods. Even during winter these traditional varieties need to be outside. In colder climates this can mean burying the pot in the ground and mulching or otherwise covering the bonsai to protect it from freezing temperatures. Thus in the middle of winter, when those in cold climates most crave the presence of green plants to nourish their memories and dreams of summer, their treasured bonsai are tucked away under protection and out of sight.

Traditional bonsai uses long-lived trees that can survive for hundreds of years and take generations to develop. Fifteen- to thirty-year-old specimens can look very nice, but truly impressive bonsai are often 125 to 250 years old or older. This requires several generations of training and is an important component of traditional bonsai culture and philosophy. Even a bonsai trained for only five to twenty-five years can cost hundreds of dollars. The long period of development is a major factor in discouraging more widespread practice of this art among today's society, which seems to want instant gratification for any effort. Moreover, complicated training techniques, such as root-pruning and branch wiring, are intimidating to the novice and are enough to scare many people entirely away from this art.

Although this concept of great age and long work spans may be integral to traditional bonsai philosophy, it is possible to train beautiful, mature specimens in only one year using nontraditional methods and plant varieties such as the various herbs. Herbs have occasionally been used as bonsai subjects, although they are usually considered an oddity. But using many different herbs as subjects extends the art of bonsai into a new dimension that makes this beautiful tradition more accessible to novice enthusiasts.

Herbs offer many advantages when it comes to bonsai training. They are easy to grow, for one. Because herbs grow on a different time scale than traditional trees, a well-developed woody trunk can be grown from a small plant in a short period of time. By using the field-growing method outlined in this book, a "mature" bonsai can be created in one growing season—less than a year—and can then be maintained and refined for many years to come. And though some herbs are hardy and can be kept outdoors year-round, most will also survive quite well indoors in a bright window. Finally, many of the best herbs, such as rosemary, seem to naturally grow in a twisted, gnarled manner that creates beautiful wild tree shapes without wiring, although wire can often be used later to refine the original shape.

Herbs are also easy to acquire. They can be propagated by seeds or cuttings. Herbs can be bought inexpensively at garden centers or from mail-order catalogs. Some of the best potential specimens may even be found in your own garden or a friend's.

The variety of scents herbs offer add new delight to growing bonsai. Trimming a rosemary plant in the house will fill a room with a pleasant fragrance. Herbal bonsai do not require time-consuming trimming. Even with relatively fast-growing herbs, five or ten minutes once every month or two is enough to keep your bonsai in good shape. There's no messy pine sap to deal with or sharp needles to lose in the carpet. Best of all, the trimmings removed from each specimen can be used for cooking, brewing tea, or making potpourri. I often make herbal jellies and wines from bonsai trimmings.

In short, there is no better way to learn about bonsai than using herbs as your first subject. They are inexpensive, so there is little financial risk as compared with purchasing a trained bonsai worth hundreds of dollars. They grow quickly, so a "mature" bonsai can be created in less than a year from a small plant or in hours from an already mature herb plant. This quicker growth also means a faster response to trimming and shaping, which allows the novice to learn quickly how a bonsai responds to training techniques. Finally, the trimmings removed from your herbal bonsai are useful and even good for you. So don't wait. Find yourself an herbal subject and start your herbal bonsai collection today.

FOR TEACHERS

Because of their ease in transplanting and the quick response to pruning, herbs are the ideal material to use in teaching bonsai classes. Herbs are inexpensive and easily replaceable, and the students will see almost immediate results from their work. New growth will appear within days, and this quick response is gratifying to the learner. The perception of bonsai as a difficult, time-consuming process that takes years to see results keeps many people from pursuing this fascinating art form. Using fast-growing herbs to introduce this art to prospective enthusiasts will do much to increase participation in the art of bonsai. And because most newcomers to bonsai are looking for a tree to keep as a houseplant, it is a great disservice to the art to start someone with a traditional hardy tree that will likely die before any results are seen.

Using a large herbal stock plant to create an "instant" bonsai makes an excellent demonstration when explaining the art of bonsai. I have done this to demonstrate bonsai on television, at lectures, and in classrooms. Many people are afraid to prune their plants, and the drastic pruning undertaken when training a large container-grown plant as explained in chapter 7 makes a dramatic impression on an audience. It will likely take hours the first time someone tries it, but with experience a beautiful bonsai can be carved out of a large rosemary in less than thirty minutes.

2

Selecting the Right Herb

So you've decided to train herbs as bonsai. Where do you begin? There are hundreds of herb varieties, a large number of which can be trained in the bonsai tradition. They can range from 4-inch miniature specimens to large-leaved "trees" over 3 feet tall. Some ground-cover varieties make good companion plants to accent your herbal bonsai (see chapter 9). A few herbs occasionally have been trained by classic growers. Pictures of oregano and rosemary are shown as oddities in some traditional bonsai books. Herbs that I have studied as bonsai subjects can be roughly divided into groups based upon their growth characteristics and environmental needs: tender perennial shrubs, tender perennials, annuals, semihardy perennials, and hardy perennials. Thymes (*Thymus* spp.) and scented geraniums (*Pelargonium* spp.) also should be considered as separate groups.

The varieties you start with will depend on your personal preferences and on which plants are available at your local greenhouse or are already growing in your garden, although you may wish to mail-order from a specialized nursery. A few varieties are easier to work with. Rosemary is probably the best choice for a first attempt at bonsai: It can form a woody shrub, is easy to obtain and care for, and resembles traditional pines. Lemon verbena and sweet bay (laurel) are true woody shrub-trees that can reach 10 to 40 feet in their native habitats. As such, they are closest to traditional bonsai subjects and may be the first choice for experienced bonsai enthusiasts. Scented geraniums, which grow quickly and are easy to care for, make another good choice for a first subject. Don't be afraid to try anything, especially if you already have a suitable subject, but the above varieties are easiest to work with.

TENDER PERENNIAL SHRUBS

A number of true trees are labeled as herbs in some herbal books because of their medicinal uses. These include willows, junipers, barberries, hawthorns, black cherry, oaks, and citrus species, among others. Junipers are used extensively in traditional bonsai but aren't considered herbs by most people. Although not the main subject of this book, a few of these species deserve mention because they are easy to grow as houseplants and make exceptional bonsai. Various **citrus species** are attractive trees that are available in garden centers all over the country. The best variety for use as bonsai is the calamondin orange (*Citrus mitis*), which is a cross between the mandarin orange (*Citrus reticulata*) and the Nagami kumquat (*Fortunella margarita*). The small fruits are excellent for use in cooking and making preserves and will hold on the tree for months. The flowers have the wonderful fragrance of all the citrus trees.

Olive trees (*Olea europaea*) have a long tradition in human history. These long-lived, slow-growing trees can do well as houseplants. A number of dwarf varieties grown as ornamentals in this country will make attractive bonsai. Their only disadvantage, other than slow growth similar to traditional bonsai trees, is that most of these ornamentals are non-fruiting. Fruiting varieties are hard to find, and the fruit (and its oil) is the part of the tree with herbal uses.

Pomegranate (*Punica granatum*) is another plant with a long tradition of use as food and medicine. There are many varieties with different colored flowers, and some have variegated foliage. Pomegranates need cool night temperatures under 65 degrees F. (18 degrees C.) through the winter and will lose their leaves for a month or two at that time. This period of rest will keep them vigorous for many years. The leaves are brilliant yellow in the fall and have red tints in the new growth. The best variety for bonsai is the dwarf pomegranate (*P. granatum* 'Nana'), which flowers freely and forms 1- to 2-inch miniature fruits.

Perhaps the best candidate for bonsai in this group is **dwarf sweet myrtle** (*Myrtus communis compacta*), a handsome small shrub with fragrant dark green foliage that was used historically as a strewing herb because of its sweet odor. Mentioned in the Old Testament of the Bible, it has a long tradition of ceremonial use in garlands, wreaths, and bouquets for every occasion, and as crowns upon the brow of returning war heroes. Modern uses include potpourri and scenting bath water. *M.c.* 'Microphylla', another dwarf variety, has a variegated form that creates a strikingly beautiful bonsai. Display this bright-colored

This sweet myrtle grove has eleven trees and a central rock of mica schist studded with gem garnet and staurolite crystals. The photo was taken one month after planting.

myrtle, with its light green leaves with creamy yellow edges, against a dark background for a spectacular appearance. The tiny, pointed leaves of any of the myrtles are in perfect scale for use in bonsai and look especially good planted in groves. Myrtle's starry white flowers are quite fragrant and under good conditions will develop into small blue-black berries that keep for months when left on the bush.

For the main focus of this book, however, only plants I have worked with that would commonly be considered herbs will be discussed. For our purposes, tender perennial shrubs will include lemon verbena, sweet bay laurel, and rosemary. These are long-lived species that can be expected to live for thirty or more years but will not survive subfreezing temperatures.

Lemon verbena (*Aloysia triphylla,* formerly *Lippia citriodora*) is a large shrub or small tree that can reach more than 10 feet tall. Though its leaves are rather large, they are narrow and can make an attractive bonsai. This tree is deciduous and will drop its leaves every winter. Leaf drop also can be stimulated by any drastic shock, such as moving a specimen indoors or a severe change in temperature. The dormant period usually lasts from one to three months and provides a seasonal change for viewing as does traditional deciduous bonsai. New plants are relatively easy to start from cuttings during warm weather or if kept over 65 degrees F. (18 degrees C.). Under good conditions, lemon verbena can grow 3 to 6 feet during a single growing season when planted in the ground. For this reason it must be trimmed regularly during the summer in order to develop a good shape. Lemon verbena likes warm weather, should be dug and potted earlier in the fall than most other herbs, and will tolerate a warm spot inside the house during the winter. Watch for insects during the winter period. Spider mites and white flies are both attracted to lemon verbena.

Sweet bay laurel (*Laurus nobilis*) is an aromatic evergreen shrub that can reach more than 40 feet in height when planted in the ground in warm regions. Despite this, it is a slow-growing plant that will grow only a few inches per year when potted, although it may grow 3 to 4 feet in a season when field-planted. Bay is not easy to propagate; cuttings take a long time to root and seeds are difficult to germinate. For the best start, buy a small plant in time to plant outside for the growing season. Bay is long-lived and can be developed for many years as a bonsai. Under good growing conditions, it has a tendency to throw side shoots or suckers, which must be removed to keep the bonsai shape. Bay likes warm conditions indoors and requires bright light. During winter in the house, bay needs a warm south window and will benefit from additional artificial lighting.

Rosemary (*Rosmarinus officinalis*) is perhaps the best herb to grow as a bonsai. It's widely available, is easy to grow, survives well in pots kept indoors, and resembles traditional pines. Rosemary is long-lived compared with many other herbs and can be kept alive for thirty years or more. When field-grown, rosemary grows quickly and gets quite woody. Starting with small plants purchased from a local greenhouse, I have grown magnificent bonsai specimens with trunks more than 1 inch in diameter during a single growing season. There are a number of rosemary varieties. Flowers can be dark blue, light blue, pink, or white, and there are different types of foliage, including variegated. There is even a pine-scented variety.

Seeds are slow to germinate, and the young plants grow very slowly. Cuttings are the best way to propagate, and the only way for some unusual varieties. Rosemary will benefit from some trimming during the summer growing season, but nice specimens can still be obtained from plants that are neglected until they are dug in the fall. Rosemary tolerates cool conditions and can survive in an east, south, or west window during the winter. Avoid using too much peat in potting soils for rosemary, as it thrives in well-drained alkaline soils. Keeping the roots too wet is damaging, although they must not be allowed to completely dry out. Using more sand and less peat in the soil will help with both of these problems. Rosemary is also subject to powdery mildew, a white fuzzy growth that attacks the leaves. Keeping the plant warmer and drier and increasing air circulation around your rosemary will alleviate this condition. Despite these problems, rosemary is easy to grow indoors and is my favorite herbal bonsai subject.

There are several varieties of **creeping or prostrate rosemary** (*Rosmarinus officinalis* 'Prostratus'), of which Santa Barbara rosemary is perhaps the most attractive. Environmental needs and care are similar to those of the upright rosemaries. These varieties can be developed in a cascade style in which the growing tip of the plant extends below the bottom of the pot, reminiscent of a tree growing down from a cliff. Because of their trailing habit, special care must be taken during the field-growing period. If these plants are allowed to lie in the dirt during this period, they will lose a lot of their attractiveness. When growing these varieties in a flat garden space, surround the plant with flat rocks, tiles, or pieces of thin lumber to keep the growing plant off the dirt. For best results in training a cascade-style bonsai, plant the specimen on the edge of a raised bed where it can trail over the edge. A cascading rosemary is one of the most beautiful of all herbal bonsai.

TENDER PERENNIALS

Tender perennials will live for years and can get quite woody, although they are not considered true woody shrubs. They like warm conditions and bright light. A bright south window is the best winter location for these bonsai, but they will survive in an east or west window. Though they like warmth, these species will tolerate lower temperatures and will even survive temporary drops to the upper thirties (near 0 degrees C). Prostrate rosemary should probably be considered as part of this group, although I've included it with the upright rosemary under Tender Perennial Shrubs.

French lavender (*Lavandula dentata*) is a graceful plant with indented leaves that gets quite woody and can be grown in either upright or cascading styles. It makes a beautiful bonsai that can live for years. Flowers arch on long stems with a hoplike head and fragrant light purple flowers. With bright enough light, it can bloom throughout the winter. New growth is pale green and somewhat weak under low-light conditions. French lavender has a tendency to droop and can be grown upright or wired to cascade until the stems harden as they turn woody. This variety needs brighter sun, a little more water, and richer soils than the more common lavenders. Seeds are slow to germinate and slow to grow after germination. Cuttings will take at all times of the year and are the best way to propagate this plant. Probably because of its strongly scented oils, it is seldom bothered by insect pests, although white flies may take to it.

As it matures, sweet marjoram acquires a tough, craggy wood that is essential in bonsai. This specimen is three years old..

Spanish lavender (*Lavandula stoechas*) has smaller leaves with a silvery green color. It won't grow as lush as the French variety and will better tolerate dryness. It is more difficult to grow indoors than the French species. At two to three years old, Spanish lavender can appear very aged with great character. This lavender is smaller than the French species. Any of the *Lavandula* genus make good bonsai subjects.

Sweet marjoram (*Origanum majorana*) is a delicate plant that is often considered to be an annual but is a true perennial that develops nice wood as it ages. New growth forms as green shoots up to 1 foot long that become woody when the plant begins to flower. On a mature bonsai specimen, these shoots must be closely trimmed or removed entirely unless you wish to change the entire architecture of the bonsai. Brighter light during the winter will keep this new growth from being too weak as it stretches for the light. Although considered tender, sweet marjoram can survive cool temperatures and even a light frost. Seeds germinate rapidly and cuttings are quick to root, making this plant easy to propagate. Sweet marjoram has a delightful fragrance and delicate appearance. It is one of the best herbs for quickly developing an aged, gnarled appearance characteristic of the oldest, most valued of the traditional bonsai. It will also be one of the smallest in scale; a mature specimen often is only 6 to 8 inches high while appearing to be very old.

Pineapple sage (*Salvia elegans*) is a large, vigorous plant that grows on an entirely different scale from a miniature like sweet marjoram. A mature pineapple sage bonsai will be 2 to 3 feet tall. With this size, the large leaves will not be too much out of scale. This plant gets rather large before becoming woody; a field-grown bush may be 4 to 5 feet tall before it is cut back to develop a bonsai. Pineapple sage likes it warm and sunny; the first light frost will kill it if left outside too long. It blooms late in the year as the days shorten. A mature specimen or a first-year bonsai (if shaped early enough) will often produce a showy display of bright red, tubular flowers from fall through midwinter. This alone makes this large plant desirable to train as a bonsai. Another benefit is the pineapple-scented foliage that makes this plant a joy to trim and flavors a delightful herbal tea. These attractive features make pineapple sage, which might otherwise be considered too large, a desirable herbal bonsai that provides an interesting counterpoint to miniature herbal bonsai like thyme or sweet marjoram.

Lion's ear (*Leonotis Leonuris*) is a vigorous shrub with bright green foliage and orange flowers. Though it can reach 6 feet or more when grown in the field, lion's ear is easily trimmed into a nice bonsai and makes an impressive specimen. The leaves are larger than those of most other herbs but much smaller than those of pineapple sage. The trunk thickens quickly, and the well-developed root system will need a large pot.

Curry plant (*Helichrysum angustifolium*) is a small shrub with bright silver foliage, a strong scent, and yellow buttonlike flowers in season. Leaves are small, and the metallic color creates a distinctive bonsai that commands attention. This plant has a tendency to throw strong suckers from the trunk and branches. This vigorous growth should be removed as soon as it shows to encourage growth at the branch tips. This plant is not used to make the cooking spice and is definitely not recommended for internal consumption. Use the trimmings and flowers for dried arrangements, herbal wreaths, and sachets to protect clothes from moths.

Costa Rican mint bush (*Satureja viminea*) is a plant I've just recently begun to work with, yet it's quickly becoming one of my favorites. A fast grower that becomes woody at an early age, this bush will send up suckers from the roots at the base of the trunk. These should be removed as soon as they show. The bright lime green leaves stand out from a distance and give off a strong minty aroma when bruised. This is one of the most attractive plants I've worked with. It grows throughout the Caribbean, where it is used to flavor meat dishes.

ANNUALS

It seems strange to even consider annuals as subjects for bonsai because these plants may live only one to three years. Still, they can be developed into what appears as a mature bonsai in just three to six months. Growing these plants will help you appreciate differing life spans, which is important in the philosophy underlying bonsai tradition, especially with the difference that herbs bring to this art form.

These plants like very warm conditions and can suffer serious shock from sudden temperature changes. They can be grown entirely in pots without the field-growing period recommended for other herbs. This is a good method of growing these herbs as bonsai, since they also are subject to transplant shock, which can kill them. Summer savory and various basils are the prime members of this group.

A number of **basils** can be trained as bonsai. Bush basil (*Ocimum basilicum minimum*) is the best variety to use because of its small leaves and miniature habit. Camphor basil (*O. kilimandscharicum*) is a true perennial that will live longer than the annual basils, although it is larger in scale. This variety should be planted in a pot without growing in the field, as it suffers severe transplant shock if moved into a pot and brought indoors. Opal basil (*O. basilicum 'Purpurascens'*) makes an unusual and attractive bonsai. Lemon basil (*O. basilicum citriodorum*) and cinnamon basil (*O. Basilicum* cv) are delightful herbs with wonderful fragrances and make exotic cooking spices. These are worth growing as bonsai just to keep a ready supply of fresh leaves on hand for use in the kitchen. Most other basils also will work, except for lettuce leaf basil (*O. basilicum 'Crispum'*), which has leaves much too large to look good as a bonsai. Basil likes hot and humid conditions, is extremely frost sensitive, and will not grow well if temperatures drop into the forties or fifties (near 10 degrees C). In spite of its short life, basil can make a very unusual bonsai.

Summer savory (*Satureja hortensis*) is a fast-growing, bushy plant that needs a lot of trimming to shape as a bonsai. It has a tendency to get top-heavy and must be thinned by removing some branches entirely and cutting back those branches that remain. Summer savory is easily started from seed and grows rapidly. It can take cooler temperatures than the basils but needs bright light or winter growth will be too weak and won't stand up. It is also subject to drying out and needs frequent watering. This plant doesn't get as woody as other herbs but can still be developed into a nice bonsai.

SEMIHARDY PERENNIALS

Semihardy perennials will tolerate frost and light freezes but will not survive hard freezes like most hardy herbs. They will also tolerate warmer indoor conditions than most of the hardy perennials. They can be wintered indoors or outside where temperatures seldom go below 25 degrees F. (-5 degrees C.). The santolinas in this group are interesting herbal bonsai subjects because of their vigorous growth, wide tolerance for different environmental conditions, and unusual fragrance. Winter savory and germander round out this group.

There are two species of **santolina,** or lavender cotton, that work very well as bonsai subjects. Gray santolina (*Santolina chamaecyparissus*) has beautiful soft foliage with an almost woolly appearance and narrow, fringed leaves. Green santolina (*S. virens*) has bright, shiny green leaves that are so narrow they appear threadlike. The two have similar environmental needs, although the green variety will survive colder temperatures. Santolina likes bright light and will look best in a southern exposure. It will survive low-light conditions such as an east window through the winter but will send out lots of weak growth that stretches for the light. A regular "haircut" will keep your specimen in shape. Santolina does well in a warm winter house and needs more water in that situation. It does even better in a cool, bright environment. Cuttings root easily and are the best method of propagation, although seeds are available too. Santolina is one of the best herbs to grow as bonsai because of its easy care and beautiful, strongly scented foliage.

Winter savory (*Satureja montana*) is an attractive evergreen plant with shiny, green leaves and a woody trunk that is green with a reddish tint. It's a small plant that can be developed into a nice bonsai only 6 to 8 inches tall. The winter savory is hardier than other members of this group and will do better if allowed a cool semidormant period in the winter. This can be accomplished by leaving the bonsai outside later in the fall while protecting it from strong freezes or by keeping it in a cool window throughout the winter. A cool window can be created with a heavy curtain that allows temperatures near freezing next to the glass and insulates this growing area from a warm house. Winter savory is slow-growing and needs less water than its annual counterpart, summer savory. It starts easily from seed and can also be propagated from cuttings. Although it is a perennial, this variety is not as long-lived as other perennial herbs and can lose its vitality after a couple of years. It is a little more difficult to grow, but its beautiful miniature appearance makes it worth the trouble.

There are several varieties of **germander** (*Teucrium chamaedrys, T. lucidum, T. scorodonia*) that make nice bonsai. All of these are upright varieties used as edging or miniature hedges. Germander has little scent and no culinary use, but this attractive plant is considered an herb because of its old medicinal uses. It prefers a cool semidormant winter and will also tolerate low-light conditions, though it should receive a little direct light. Germander is easy to propagate with seeds or cuttings and will flower easily, which makes it worth growing.

HARDY PERENNIALS

The hardy perennials are strongly scented, long-lived herbs with a number of traditional uses. Sage and oregano are culinary herbs, hyssop is medicinal, rue was a malarial and poisoning remedy, and southernwood and wormwood were used to repel insects and for expelling worms. Their scents are strong, and many have somewhat disagreeable odors with medicinal overtones. These species are evergreen and will produce larger bonsai from 1 to 2 feet high or more. They will live longer and look better if allowed a cold semidormant period. The best method for this is to leave your bonsai specimens outside late in the fall through plenty of cool weather and light freezes before bringing them into a warm house. December or January is the best time to change the environment from cold to warm. An old garden specimen can often be dug and trained into a spectacular bonsai in three to six months.

Oregano (*Origanum vulgare*) has a number of cultivars that are widely used as culinary herbs. It's a vigorous grower with a many-branched habit that requires a lot of trimming to keep in shape. Many young shoots must be removed as they bud from the bare trunk or exposed roots of an oregano bonsai. This can provide a continual supply of fresh herb to use in the kitchen, one of the best reasons for trying this plant. Because of its growth rate, it will need more water and likes brighter light than the others in this group. It is easy to start from seed or cuttings. If you have an old, established plant in the garden, you may be able to dig it in the fall and prune it severely to construct an "instant" bonsai that can look stunning after a short period of regrowth. Oregano lends itself very well to creating a many-trunked specimen or even a grove of "trees" by planting deeper instead of exposing roots. This characteristic makes oregano an interesting bonsai subject.

Sage (*Salvia officinalis*) is a vigorous, large-leaved plant that becomes quite woody as it ages. The fancy colored sages are the best varieties to train as bonsai. They are tender compared to garden sage, will do better growing in a window, and are worth growing for their variegated foliage in shades of white, purple, pink, or yellow. These varieties are propagated with cuttings, and seeds of the common sage start easily and grow fast. They need less water and tolerate low light during the winter but prefer a cool location. Sage will make a large bonsai that can stand 2 feet tall and may take several years to refine to mature form.

Rue (*Ruta graveolens*) is an attractive shrub with a strong odor, yellow flowers, and an almost metallic blue tint to its unusual divided foliage. It's very hardy and will develop into a large bonsai. Rue needs brighter light and will tolerate more heat than other members of this group, although it prefers cool winter conditions. Seeds are easy to start and grow quickly. The bright blue leaves of this herb stand in sharp contrast to the greens of other plants in a bonsai collection.

Hyssop (*Hyssopus officinalis*) is a shrubby bush often used as edging in the herb garden. It grows rapidly and can develop a strong, woody trunk in one season. It will need frequent trimming to keep in shape and should be kept in a cool, bright location through the winter to avoid unsightly weak growth. Hyssop starts quickly from seed, and an established plant can also be dug and trained easily.

Southernwood (*Artemisia abrotanum*) and **wormwood** (*A. absinthium*) are related, nearly evergreen aromatic shrubs. Southernwood's finely divided leaves are more attractive than those of wormwood. These are large, vigorous plants that can tolerate a wide variety of conditions. They are very hardy and can be wintered outside if protected like traditional bonsai. Inside, they do much better in a cool location. Both are propagated from cuttings, and a large, developed subject can often be dug out of an established clump. A large old plant can be cut to just a short stem and will sprout new little shoots, very quickly forming a crown on a woody, treelike trunk.

THYMES

At first glance, **thyme** (*Thymus* spp.) would seem the ideal bonsai candidate. Its tiny leaves and delicate appearance provide perhaps the best scale for miniature bonsai, and there are innumerable forms to choose from. There are enough differences in colors and patterns of variegation, leaf shape and size, fragrance, and flower color to make an entire collection of various thymes. **Golden lemon thyme** (*T. citriodorus* 'Aureus') and **silver thyme** (*T. citriodorus* 'Argenteus') are perhaps the most attractive thymes because of the beautiful bright yellow ('Aureus') and stark white ('Argenteus') variegation and the strong lemon scent of the golden form. Caraway thyme (*T. herba-barona*), with its distinctive odor and tiny leaves, can often be carved into an "instant" bonsai from an established plant. Although caraway thyme is considered a creeper, an old plant can have a finger-size trunk that will create a spectacular miniature bonsai only 4 to 6 inches tall.

Thyme is the most difficult herb to train as bonsai, however. The detailed structure requires tedious work to keep in shape, but the main problem is thyme's susceptibility to transplant shock. It is difficult to move from the field into a pot. The loss rate when doing this in the fall can run as high as 50 percent. Risk can be reduced by using larger pots and less severe root-pruning than other species. Another option is to grow thyme in a pot rather than the field during the early phases of its training. It's always possible to lose a specimen when using the drastic measures recommended in this book, but thyme seems to have a higher loss rate than any other herb I've trained. Plan for this by growing extra plants and accepting some loss. Once potted, thyme should never be field-grown again and should be repotted only once a year in the spring. It prefers a bright location in the house, and although it likes well-drained soil and dry climates, thyme must be watered carefully and regularly in the home. It's all too easy for it to dry out and die from shock, especially if subject to warm drafts in the winter house. Despite these difficulties, thyme is worth the effort because of its tiny leaves, many forms, and delightful fragrances.

SCENTED GERANIUMS

The **scented geraniums** (*Pelargonium* spp.) constitute a large group of species and cultivars that are simple to grow, survive well on the windowsill, and are easily trained as bonsai. There are more than two hundred species and countless cultivars of scented geraniums. Some of the varieties I've worked with are lemon (*P. crispum*), lime (*P. nervosum*), ginger (*P. torento*), nutmeg (*P. fragrans*), rose (*P. graveolens*), gooseberry (*P. grossularioides*), strawberry (*P. scabrum*), fern-leaf (*P. filicifolium*), and peppermint (*P. tomentosum*). Many others are suitable; those with small leaves work best. Peppermint has a large leaf but can be developed into a dramatic cascade specimen that hangs 3 feet below the pot. Lemon is one of the best to train because of its small, bright green leaves. The 'Prince Rupert' variety of lemon has bright yellow-variegated foliage that makes a beautiful, attention-getting bonsai.

Geraniums like bright light and plenty of water. Their fast growth rate requires frequent trimming but is perfect for training bonsai. Regrowth is rapid after trimming, and you will see results from your training techniques in just a few weeks. Because of this rapid growth, old leaves yellow quickly, as with all geraniums. Heavy fertilizing will slow this process somewhat, but all scented geraniums will need to have yellow leaves removed often. Save these leaves to make a strong-scented potpourri.

Scented geraniums can be transplanted frequently without problems, but they must be allowed to become slightly root-bound in the pot if you want them to flower. Some scented geraniums can be started from seed, although most are propagated from cuttings. Their easy care and delightful fragrance can make scented geraniums the most enjoyable of all herbs to work with.

3

TRAINING YOUR HERBAL BONSAI CANDIDATE

THE FIRST STEP in developing your herbal bonsai is to acquire the plant you wish to train. Next, you'll give it an initial trimming, then plant it outdoors and let it grow for one season, so that the trunk can mature.

Many herbs, such as rosemary, thyme, sweet marjoram, and basil, can be started from seed. It can be immensely satisfying to grow bonsai from seed all the way to a mature specimen. Herbs offer you the chance to do this and have a beautiful bonsai one to three years after sowing seed. Starting seed is the best way to propagate basil, especially if you want one of the more exotic varieties. In warm conditions, basil starts easily and grows quickly. Other herbs, notably lavender and rosemary, are slow to germinate and grow slowly for the first year. They can be propagated much more quickly from cuttings.

FROM CUTTINGS

Many herbs, such as most scented geraniums, can be propagated only from cuttings. This is not a difficult process if done properly. Cuttings should be 3 to 6 inches long, with the leaves stripped off the lower half of each stem. Soft cuttings like scented geraniums are best rooted in a soilless germinating medium. Dip the geranium cuttings in rooting hormone, then set them aside in the shade for 6 to 12 hours to wilt and facilitate callus formation. When using soilless mediums, obtain a commercial plug tray from a garden center, or use

Propagation from cuttings expedites the growth process of many herbs.

2- to 3-inch pots. Wet the medium thoroughly, stick in the cuttings, and place in a bright window or under lights. Set up a plastic tent greenhouse or mist the cuttings to keep humidity high. Roots will form in one to three months. Most herbs can be rooted this way.

Another method, which doesn't work well with geraniums, involves filling a nursery tray or a wide, shallow bulb pot with a mixture of four parts coarse builder's sand and one part each perlite and vermiculite. Dip the cuttings in rooting hormone, and place them in rows in the sand flat. This system needs good drainage and must be watered frequently, but the cuttings can quickly form vigorous root balls that transplant well and grow quickly. This is my preferred method of rooting herb cuttings other than geraniums. Cuttings are a good method of propagating plants, especially unusual varieties, but there is no need to grow your own bonsai from cuttings or seed.

SMALL PLANTS

Perhaps the best way to grow your bonsai is to start with a small plant that already has a pleasing shape and develop it from there. Many varieties of herbs can be purchased at local garden centers. Using well-developed young plants gives you a head start in developing your bonsai. The advantage of using your local garden center is that you can sort through a large number of plants and pick out specimens with well-developed or unusual trunks. There can be a big difference between plants in the same tray, so take your time and choose your candidates carefully. Pick out a couple of extra plants. It's not at all unusual to lose a plant or two during the training process described in this book, and if you end up with an extra bonsai, it will make a excellent gift someday.

There are a number of mail-order nurseries that sell hundreds of rare and unusual herbs (see References and Resources). More than one hundred varieties of scented geraniums alone can be obtained from specialty nurseries. But you won't have the luxury of hundreds of plants to choose from—you get what they send. Their description (and your imagination) of the herb variety may not match the plant's appearance when it arrives, and some experiments may not work. But take a chance: There are many obscure varieties waiting to be discovered as potential bonsai. Costa Rican mint bush and variegated sweet myrtle are two of my favorite successes that were obtained by mail order, sight unseen.

MATURE PLANTS

A faster way to create a bonsai, although you have less control over its basic style, is to start with a larger plant. Look for a 1- or 2-gallon stock plant with a thick, well-developed trunk and branch architecture. This plant may already be several years old. A plant like this can be trimmed into a beautiful bonsai at one sitting, as will be shown in chapter 7. Herbs this size can be bought from mail-order nurseries, but your best bet is to visit as many garden centers as possible and talk to employees about what you want. Not every place will have herbs this large, but some will, and it is quite possible to find old plants on sale when a nursery decides to get rid of old stock. There are some large wholesale nurseries that ship all over the country and carry popular herbs such as rosemary, lavender, and santolina in 1- to 5-gallon sizes. Your local nursery can order these for you.

It's best, however, to have a selection of plants to look through. You will need to find a plant that already has an attractive shape with nice branches, because it will be too late to develop the bonsai's main structure. Plants that were used as stock plants have been trimmed regularly, and many of them will have nice shapes for development as bonsai. You will have to work with what you get, but some of these old stock plants can be shaped into spectacular bonsai that look beautiful as soon as you finish trimming.

One last source for finding your bonsai candidate should not be overlooked. A plant with potential for becoming a beautiful bonsai may be hiding right under your nose. Existing herb gardens often have several gnarled old plants that could be trained into beautiful bonsai. As fast as herbs grow, any herb plant over one year old is a potential candidate. If you have been growing herbs for a year or more, you probably already have a good plant to work with. So check your garden, or work out a deal with a friend—offer to trade plants or train two bonsai and give one back to your friend. If you have grown tender herbs such as rosemary or scented geraniums in pots, these will make ideal candidates for training as bonsai. Herbs that are already potted are easier to work with and suffer less transplant shock than field-grown plants.

DESIRABLE CHARACTERISTICS

When selecting a small plant to grow in the field, the shape of the trunk is important, but directing the future growth of the bonsai is the main consideration. Almost every plant with any shape can be directed to grow into a beautiful bonsai with the right pruning and, if necessary, wiring. Look for a sturdy trunk with strong roots and a pleasing shape. There are several basic shapes or styles to consider when looking at a potential bonsai and trying to imagine its future growth. Formal upright, slanting, and cascade styles are the main shapes, of which there are many variations.

There are also a couple of less common styles that work well with herbal bonsai. Double- and multiple-trunk bonsai can be quite striking, and many herbs send up strong new

Beautiful in its simplicity, the formal upright is one of the most popular bonsai styles.

shoots from the base that can be trained in this style. If your plant has suitable shoots already, you can simply trim the trunk above these shoots and plant the remaining trunk and

Ornate and elegant, the slanting bonsai works well in arrangements with rocks and ground cover.

For a touch of drama, bonsai can be trained in a cascade style.

bases of the shoots at ground level. Don't trim the tips of the shoots; you want them to grow straight without branching to develop strong parallel trunks that will give your multiple-trunk bonsai good form. They can be cut back severely at a later time to begin developing a crown above the strong trunks. Costa Rican mint bush is probably the best example of this type of herb and is easily trained as a multiple-trunk bonsai. In fact, this variety sends out new shoots so strongly that it needs to have the new shoots removed quite often, several times a month if you wish to keep multiple trunks from forming.

The root-over-rock style can be quite striking, and field-growing an herbal bonsai is the ideal method of developing this style. You will need to select a vigorous plant with a well-developed root structure. After trimming the plant to the desired shape, wash away the dirt from the base of the trunk and the area where the main roots separate. See chapter 9 for a

Certain herbs will develop shoots at their bases that can be trained to grow into second trunks, or double-trunk bonsai.

*Allow several shoots to grow at the base of an herb to create
multiple-trunk bonsai.*

discussion of collecting and using the appropriate types of rock. Your chosen rock should
be placed under the base of the trunk and the roots wrapped around the rock before the
plant and rock are planted in the field. The rock should be placed at the surface of the soil
so that the growing tips of the roots will develop below the rock. If necessary, mound dirt
around the edges of the rock to cover the root tips until they grow deeper. The roots will
grow right around the rock and become exposed when the bonsai is dug up to be placed in a
pot for training.

When choosing a large plant for creating an "instant" bonsai, look at the current shape
and branch development of the plant. A large, well-developed plant is unlikely to perfectly
fit one of the classic styles, but by paying attention to balance and flow in the structure of
the plant, you can create a strikingly beautiful bonsai with a nontraditional shape. Look at a
large number of plants if you can; there will be great variation in shapes available. It is not
hard to find older plants that can be carved into spectacular bonsai in a couple of hours.

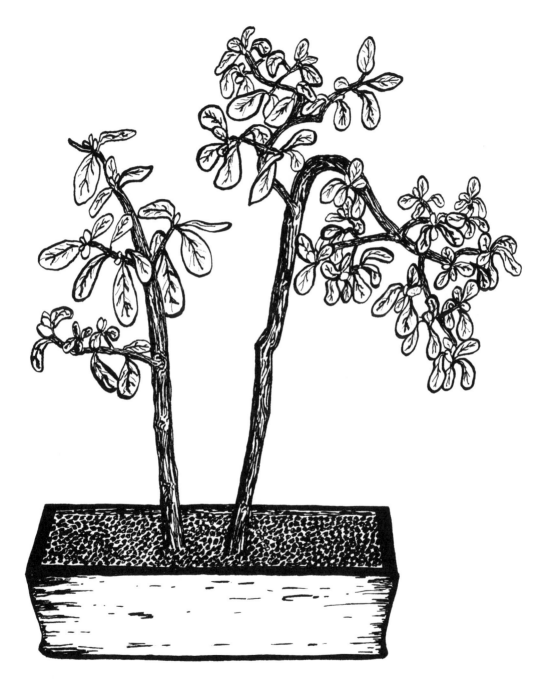

This Costa Rican mint bush is planted deep with a pair of shoots trained in double-trunk style.

An unusual, mysterious bonsai is achieved through the root-over-rock method.

Push aside the foliage to examine the plants' internal structure. Look for large, well-balanced branches that will create a pleasing shape when all the undesirable branches have been removed. You will need to remove many branches from the typical specimen. Herbs send out new shoots constantly on the trunk and thick branches. A large specimen will have many little branches that, until removed, can hide the appearance of the trunk and main branches. (Chapter 7 provides instructions on trimming a large container-grown herb plant.)

Check below the soil line, too. Tap the root ball out of the pot and examine it. Plants that have been container-grown are often planted deep when repotted, and much of the trunk will be below ground level. You may have to remove some small roots, but many herbs have the most dramatic part of the trunk buried under ground level. I have exposed 4 to 6 inches of trunk on a 1- or 2-gallon stock plant to create a dramatic base for some marvelous bonsai.

THE INITIAL TRIMMING

Even if your plant is well grown and quite bushy, you will need to reduce it to its basic structure of a trunk and three or four main branches. Remove all extra branches, leaving what will be the basic skeleton of your bonsai. The branches that are left should be trimmed at the point you wish them to branch. The strongest new shoots will form at the point where the branch is trimmed. Shoots will form lower on the branch closer to the trunk, but these will be weaker and will eventually be removed. Be careful if wiring a small plant that is to be field-planted; herbs grow rapidly when field-planted and will grow into and be scarred by wire very quickly. If you decide to wire, use thicker wire, wrap it loosely, and keep a close eye on the plant during the growing season. You will likely need to remove the wire sometime before the growing season is over, well before your bonsai is dug and placed into a pot.

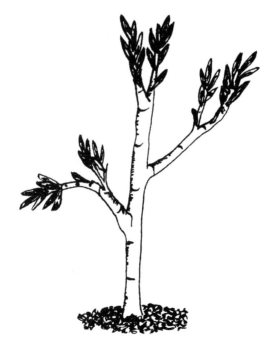

An early trimming of the branches will ensure the growth of stonger, new shoots.

PLANTING OUT

Field-planting for a season will cause dramatic thickening of the trunk and is the method used to grow dramatic bonsai in a shorter period of time. Traditional woody trees are often field-planted for several years to promote trunk and root development. Because of the faster growth rate of herbs, one season (late spring through early fall) of field growth will be as dramatic as five to fifteen years of field-growing woody trees like elm, maple, or pine.

Field-planting your herbal bonsai is the fastest way to develop the trunk and produce an aged look. This can be as simple as planting your pretrimmed bonsai candidate in your garden. Herbs prefer full sun. They will survive in partial shade, but to obtain the best growth with tight, short internode spacing, your herbal bonsai should be planted out in full sun.

In order to reduce transplant shock when digging your field-grown plant after the growing season, the soil in your planting field should be amended so that it is similar to the potting soil you will use when potting your field-grown bonsai. (See chapter 5 for a discussion of potting soils.) All field soils will benefit from the addition of compost or peat, and any potting soil will have some type of organic matter in it, most likely peat. Most herbs prefer alkaline soils, so if you add much peat, which is somewhat acidic, you need to balance the acidity by adding some agricultural lime. Herbs also prefer well-drained soil, so mix some coarse sand or perlite into the soil at your planting site.

Raised beds are a good way to improve drainage, especially in wet climates. In drier climates, you will need to water more often if you use raised beds. This is also a good method for growing herbs in the cascade style. Bonsai grown in cascade or semicascade style must be protected from lying in the dirt. If you don't have a raised bed constructed of wood or stone, you can still shield your plants from the dirt by using tiles, boards, or flat stones for the plant to rest on. I grew a crop of semicascade rosemaries once by staking out a piece of weed barrier cloth and planting the young rosemaries in slits cut in the cloth. This kept the growing plants out of the dirt and saved considerable labor when it came to weeding. The labor saving was especially important because those rosemaries were part of a crop of three hundred herbal bonsai I was growing that summer.

A cascade bonsai can also be grown in a tall pot rather than in the field. Unless you have a tall raised bed, this is probably the best way to train a true cascade that will hang far below the bottom of your pot. Use a large pot, much larger than the final pot your cascade herbal bonsai will make its home in. You want to simulate field conditions during this initial growing season in order to maximize growth and trunk development.

Field-grown plants will always grow more than plants that are confined to a pot. That is why the best way to develop an herbal bonsai in one season is to grow it in the field. The

This young gooseberry-scented geranium is ready to be shaped. Geraniums should be reduced to a very simple, basic form at this stage.

The large, weak lower branch has been removed along with most of the other weaker growing tips. Several main branches and the growing tip of the crown were saved and then were trimmed in areas where branching is desired.

Young prostrate rosemary—one-year-old and ready to be shaped—can be purchased at your local nursery.

After shaping, the rosemary shows interesting features and a strong direction of movement. At the bottom of the trunk, several young shoots were retained. At least one of these should grow strong enough in the opposite direction of the others.

best way is not always the only way, however. People who live in apartments or in the city may not have a good location to field-grow an herbal bonsai. Beautiful herbal bonsai can be grown entirely in pots. It will just take longer to get the same trunk development. Use a large pot to give your bonsai-in-training lots of space to develop. It will be easy to move your bonsai to a smaller, more suitable pot when it approaches maturity. Scented geraniums in particular grow well in pots and will develop nicely in one growing season. You can shortcut this process by purchasing a large herb plant that has already grown in a pot for several years in a nursery.

4

Developing a Mature Bonsai in One Growing Season

The whole point of field-growing your herbal bonsai is to encourage rapid growth. You are developing a small plant into a specimen with a mature appearance during a three- to six-month growing season. Development of a thick trunk is the most important part of this process. Once the prebonsai is shaped and planted, the greatest trunk development will be facilitated by encouraging strong growth and not trimming the plant until it is dug in the fall after the growing season. This will also allow the branches you selected and left when initially trimming the plant to develop into thick main branches.

When it comes time to dig and trim such a plant in the fall, you will have maximum trunk and branch development. After pruning, however, your bonsai will be very stubby, and it can take another six months to a year to develop a crown that creates a finished appearance. This process can produce the most dramatic bonsai with an aged appearance. Bonsai grown in such a manner will not have a well-defined transition from thick branches through medium to small as the structure of the tree merges into the crown. The thick trunk with little definition for the transition to the crown creates the appearance of a very large, aged tree.

There are many styles of bonsai, and there is room for infinite variation within and between those styles. Different aspects of an "ideal" bonsai will be emphasized in each bonsai as its own characteristics are drawn out by your own artistic vision. A bonsai that emphasizes the trunk should not draw attention to a detailed branch structure. You probably

Trim the herb to the desired shape before planting it in the field.

Refrain from trimming the herb during growing season; this will allow for greater trunk and branch development.

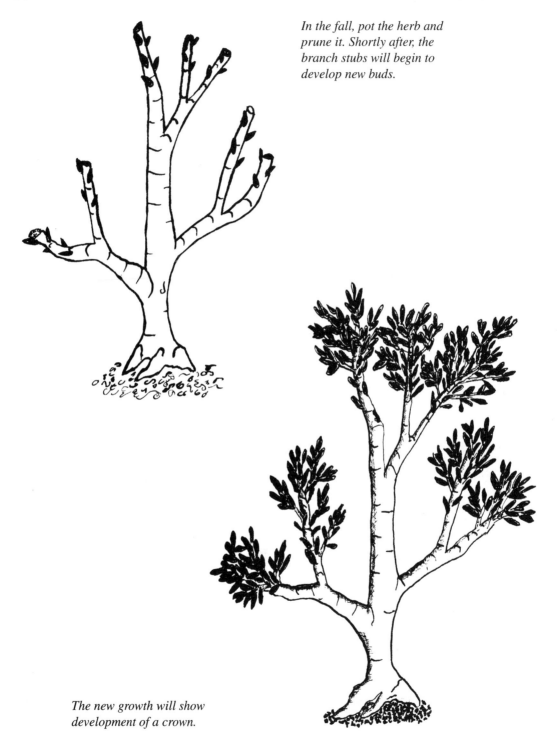

In the fall, pot the herb and prune it. Shortly after, the branch stubs will begin to develop new buds.

The new growth will show development of a crown.

had a style in mind when you planted your shaped prebonsai. By mid growing season, decisions must be made about the developing branch structure of your bonsai. A more balanced appearance will result from a midseason trim to encourage more branching, but this is done at the expense of some trunk development.

WHEN TO TRIM

Trimming during the growing season will create a bonsai with a more finished crown and a mature appearance in less time after digging your bonsai in the fall. By shaping your growing bonsai several times during the growing season, you will have a more refined specimen by fall and could possibly move your herbal bonsai straight from the field into a bonsai pot. This is the quickest way to develop a bonsai with a mature appearance. Depending on your climate, a small herb planted in April or May can be dug and planted in a nice pot by September or October, will look quite mature, and will be attractive as soon as it is potted. It can take three or four clip jobs during the summer if you want to have a "finished" bonsai at the end of the growing season. The best overall results are probably obtained by trimming only once or twice during the growing season and taking a little longer to develop the crown, although your trimming schedule will be determined by your plans for the particular bonsai. I recommend trying several different trimming schedules with your different herbal bonsai specimens to provide some variety and to determine which method gives the most pleasing results.

MAXIMIZE GROWTH

The main goal during the growing season is growth. There are many ways to fertilize plants, and everyone has his or her own preferred method. Use your usual method, and do it regularly and heavily. Foliar-application of a water-soluble 20–20–20 fertilizer works well for me. Fertilize at least once a month with stronger or more frequent applications during early and mid growing season, and taper off as you approach the end of the season.

Water is the most important factor in growing your herbal bonsai. Herbs prefer well-drained soil. In very wet climates, herbs should be planted in raised beds and extra water won't be a major consideration. In most of the country, regular watering will benefit plant growth and is even more important when using raised beds or growing in large pots. In dry climates, such as much of the interior West and Southwest, it is nearly impossible to water your plants too much. Using mulch to reduce water loss from evaporation will help conserve water and reduce plant stress caused by repeated wet-dry cycles, especially during hot and windy weather.

Growing your bonsai in large pots for the summer requires paying extra attention to the water needs of your growing herbs. Regular watering is critical, and in dry climates your growing bonsai may need daily watering during the hottest weather. Mulch can be used even in pots to reduce evaporative water loss. In dry areas with intense sun, such as higher-altitude western and southwestern parts of the country, pots should be placed where they will receive some shade during the hottest part of the day. Most herbs thrive in alkaline soils and are usually not bothered by a buildup of soluble salts. In areas with hard water, however, salt buildup from repeated watering or excessive fertilizing can damage plants. The most common sign of damage is brown leaf tips.

These salts are dissolved in the water you use to water your plants. As the water evaporates or is transpired by the plant, the salts are left behind. Repeat this dozens or hundreds of times, and a lot of salt can build up in the soil. Since these salts are soluble, the best way to remove them is to wash them out. Let's say you have an herb growing in a large pot that takes 2 to 3 quarts when you water normally. Five to 10 gallons of water should be flooded through the pot and allowed to drain over several hours. This will remove accumulated salts from hard water or overfertilization. In dry climates where plants are watered frequently with hard water, the soil should be flushed in this manner every four to six months. If you accidentally burn your plants by overfertilizing, you may be able to save them by flushing out the soil at the first sign of damage.

MIDSEASON MAINTENANCE

At midseason, your herb plant should be growing strongly and have several strong shoots or branches growing from the trimmed ends of the original plant. The trunk and main branches will be thickening and may already look quite woody. If you wired the plant after the first shaping, it is probably time to remove that wire. Check to see if the wire is scarring or in any way marking the bark of your bonsai. If so, or if the wire looks tight, remove it. Snip the wire in several places rather than trying to unwind the whole piece. If the bonsai doesn't hold its shape, rewire the branches with looser coils and bend back into the proper shape.

If the new shoots have grown 6 to 12 inches, it may be time to wire or trim them. A strong green shoot that is on the verge of turning woody will be quite flexible and can be bent into many different shapes that are easily held by wire until the shoot becomes woody and the wire is no longer needed. This is the time to create a cascade shape if that is your desire. Even varieties that grow strongly upright can be bent enough at this stage to create cascade bonsai. One of the most graceful styles of bonsai has a trunk that rises in a spiral. During the half-woody stage of your herb at midseason, wire the main shoot that will

The spiral is perhaps the most byzantine of bonsai styles.

The leaves of the lemon verbena have a triplicate whorled structure. After trimming, branches will grow in sets of three.

become the middle and upper part of the trunk, and bend this shoot into a spiral shape that will form the foundation on which you will eventually shape a crown.

Trimming the growing shoots at this point will help refine your growing bonsai and will direct the development of the crown. Each growing shoot should be trimmed at the point at which you wish it to branch, as the strongest new shoots will form right at the first internode below the cut. Most herbs have opposite leaves with each successive node rotated 90 degrees from the previous leaf node. Rosemary is a good example of this. New shoots will grow out in the direction that its basal leaf points, so the future growth of your bonsai is determined by which node is left at the tip. Lemon verbena has whorled leaves, and new branches will come out in sets of three, with each branch growing in the general direction its corresponding leaf points.

Trimming your growing bonsai like this two or three times during the growing season will give you a nicely shaped bonsai that will look good right after potting in the fall, but don't trim the plant for one to two months before moving it from the field to a pot. Remove a fair amount of foliage in order to reduce transpiration and balance the root loss that occurs at transplanting.

With specimens that are intended to have a mature appearance at the end of the growing season, use a spade to cut in a circle around the plant once or twice during the growing season to help your herbal bonsai form a small root ball. This trims the long roots and forces them to branch and grow lateral roots, resulting in a bonsai with a tight, compact root ball that is easy to dig and move directly into a bonsai pot. This root pruning will slow the overall growth of your bonsai, however, and is not necessary if you are willing to use a larger intermediate pot during the first three to six months after digging. Always combine root pruning with a trim of the foliage to balance the plant's reduced ability to take up water with a reduction in its rate of transpiration.

At the end of the growing season, your herb should be bushy with a well-developed woody trunk and strong branches. Depending on how often you trimmed your growing bonsai, the plant will either will already have a mature, finished appearance or will have a strong, well-developed trunk and basal branch structure that needs more time and work to develop a crown and a mature appearance. In either case, it's now time to move your bonsai from the field to a pot and give it closer attention.

5

POTTING YOUR FIELD-GROWN BONSAI

POTTING A FIELD-GROWN herbal bonsai specimen should be done in the fall after the growing season is over, when the weather has cooled and the plants have slowed their growth. In hot climates, it is important to wait for cooler weather to avoid shock to the plant. The root system is inevitably damaged during transplanting and loses some ability to take in water. Increased transpiration rates during hot weather can quickly kill a plant with a damaged root system.

In cooler climates, dig your subject before the first frost. Frost will kill tender varieties outright and can damage some hardy varieties. Plants could be covered and protected from light frosts if you are unable to dig them, but I see little reason to risk losing a specimen by trying to stretch the growing season. Little growth occurs at this time of the fall anyway.

Digging a field-grown plant is a harsh procedure. To minimize shock to the plants, have your pots and potting soil ready before you dig. Expect to lose some specimens during this phase of the training process. In my eighteen years of field-growing herbal bonsai, usually in the dozens or hundreds, I have seen losses ranging from zero (rarely) to more than 40 percent, with an average of 10 percent. This is why I recommend that you plant more herbs than you want to have as finished bonsai. With luck, you will end up with several extras that can be wonderful gifts for your friends.

POTTING SOIL MIXES

Basic potting soil consists of equal parts coarse sand, garden loam, and peat or compost. The key requirements are good drainage as well as water retention. Many commercial potting soils are easy to use and work well for herbal bonsai. A peat-based mix would benefit from some additional vermiculite and sand or perlite. Scented geraniums and tropical varieties, such as the Costa Rican mint bush, have high water requirements and need more water-retentive soils. Mediterranean herbs, such as lavender, rosemary, and thyme, prefer a very well drained soil and will benefit from added sand, perlite, or crushed rock. Absorbent polymers are a new product showing much promise as a water-retention aid in potting soils. These polymers look like clear crystals when dry and swell up to look and feel like gelatin cubes as they absorb water. When mixed into potting soils, these polymers are a valuable addition in dry climates, especially for small pots.

My grandmother taught me to believe in real dirt, and her greenhouse business in St. Louis used Missouri riverbottom loam in our soil mix, along with peat, sand, and perlite. In more than twenty years of commercial greenhouse work since then, I have never seen another soil that grew plants so well. I still believe in the value of good topsoil and try to use it in all my soil mixes. Not all of us are so fortunate as to live in one of the most fertile floodplains in the world, but even if you use a commercial mix, it would benefit your bonsai to add some local topsoil to it. When transplanting field-grown plants into a pot, it is especially important to use some of the same topsoil the bonsai grew in to make it easier for the roots to grow into the new soil.

POTS

Most field-grown bonsai should not be potted directly into their final display pots. A larger, intermediate pot should be used for at least three to six months before reducing the root ball once again to fit in the appropriate bonsai pot. A 6- to 10-inch pot should be suitable as an intermediate pot for most plants. In dry climates, plastic pots are preferable to unglazed clay pots, which dry out too quickly and can stress a bonsai trying to recover from the shock of transplanting.

Formal bonsai guidelines call for a pot whose depth is no more than the diameter of the trunk. This ideal is difficult to reach with a young bonsai, and it is nearly impossible when your bonsai gets transplanted into its first classic bonsai pot. Using pots shallow enough to meet classic criteria can make it difficult to keep herbal bonsai alive in dry interior environments. Pots this small will require daily watering to prevent stressing your bonsai and possibly losing it—most dead bonsai got that way by drying out.

Using a deeper, larger pot than tradition calls for makes it easier to keep bonsai alive, especially in dry climates. Fast-growing herbs need a larger pot than slow-growing hardy trees. A pot that is too small will be quickly outgrown by many herbs and will require root pruning and repotting several times a year. By decorating larger pots with ground covers and rocks (as described in chapter 9), the scene of a bonsai with its surrounding landscape will look appropriate in the larger pot. A bonsai alone, with a simple sand or moss soil cover, will be dominated by a large pot. A ground cover that reflects and complements the shape of the bonsai will draw the viewer into a landscape where the pot is forgotten and a majestic tree forms the focus of a natural scene.

A bonsai grown in the cascade style should be planted in a taller pot. The pot must be massive enough to counterbalance the weight of the tree. In order to keep the root ball small, fill the pot halfway with coarse rock and line the pot with screen before adding soil and root ball. At some point during the training of your cascade bonsai, the pot will need to be raised on a stand or placed on a shelf to keep the bonsai's crown from resting on the ground. Proper viewing of a cascade bonsai requires the pot to be placed close to eye level. This also simulates a tree in the wild growing out and down from the edge of a precipitous cliff.

POTTING UP

Your plants should be well watered the day before they are dug. If your potting soil is dry, wet it to avoid shocking your bonsai's roots. Some root damage is inevitable and will actually stimulate new root growth. In humid climates, such as eastern Missouri, where these techniques were developed, transplanting is a simple process and plants adapt easily. In dry climates like Colorado, where I currently cultivate bonsai, great care must be taken to avoid shocking the plants.

Minimize the time that bare roots are exposed to the air. Keep a spray bottle handy and mist the roots while they are exposed. Use a liquid transplant stimulator containing rooting hormones, vitamins, and nutrients when watering your newly transplanted bonsai. Several large horticultural companies produce similar products that contain root-stimulating hormones, such as 1-naphthaleneacetic acid and indole-3-butyric acid; vitamin B-1; and trace elements, such as chelated iron, manganese, and zinc. Transplant stimulators should be used in any climate and will reduce transplant shock for your bonsai.

In drier climates, don't be tempted to dig too many plants at once and then pot them up. Several times I have been tempted to cheat by digging a trayful of plants before potting any of them. Invariably this leads to loss of plants, however, because the roots are damaged by drying out. Compounding this problem, I get tempted to start shaping the bonsai by trimming away unwanted growth before it's potted because it is usually easier to see what needs to be done. I once lost forty rosemaries by getting carried away like this one afternoon. Don't dig more plants than can be comfortably shaped within an hour after potting. For your first attempt, dig and shape just one plant.

Have your pots, soil, spray bottle, and watering can (with transplant stimulator) ready. Dig out a large area around the plant to avoid severing roots. Take the root ball in your hands and crumble the dirt off while being as gentle as possible with the roots. As the roots are exposed, use the spray bottle to wash away the soil and keep the roots wet, especially the tips, which are where drying damage will occur. In dry climates, it is especially important to keep the time that roots are exposed to the air at a minimum.

The spray bottle is also useful for exposing the base of the trunk and showing where the roots divide off the base of your bonsai. This will help you determine where to place the soil level when potting the plant. Gnarled, exposed roots add greatly to the character and perceived age of a bonsai. When exposing the thick older roots, smaller undesirable roots and fine hair roots also will be exposed. If these roots will be above the new soil level of

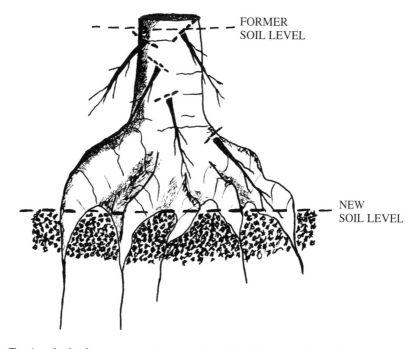

FORMER
SOIL LEVEL

NEW
SOIL LEVEL

To give the herb a more ancient, weathered look, expose the thick roots by removing the soil around the base. Trim the unwanted smaller roots.

your bonsai, they should be removed. Be careful not to remove too much root mass at this stage, however. With a bonsai that will feature a lot of large exposed roots, it may be necessary to leave some of the small, undesirable roots until the bonsai has adjusted to its new life in the intermediate pot. Leave only roots that are long enough that their tips are below the new soil level. After your bonsai has formed a new root ball and is ready to be transplanted from an intermediate pot into a bonsai pot, more of the smaller roots can be removed without too much shock to the plant.

Make sure your potting soil is slightly damp. In dry climates, roots can be desiccated by placing them in dry soil mixes. Put several inches of soil in the bottom of the pot. Place your plant's root ball in the pot, and hold the plant at the correct height to establish the new soil level. The top of the soil should be about 1 inch below the top of the pot. This makes it easier to water and take care of your bonsai. Start sifting soil into the pot all the way around the plant. Shake and tap the pot on the ground to help the soil settle. In dry climates or when worried about the moisture content of your soil, water the plant lightly when more than half the root ball is covered. Poke the soil around the roots to get rid of air pockets that can cause damage to your plant's root system; a pair of chopsticks makes an effective tool for this purpose. Fill the pot to the desired level while continuing to use chopsticks, fingers, or other tools to lightly pack the soil in place.

Water the bonsai thoroughly, giving it several waterings over twenty to thirty minutes. If you use crystal polymers in your soil mix, which I strongly recommend, they will absorb forty times their weight in water, and it will take some time for that to happen. After the initial soaking, water your bonsai several more times during the next twenty-four hours to ensure that the soil and polymers are saturated. After the soil has settled, you may need to add or take away small amounts to establish the proper soil level for the best display of your bonsai.

To ease the shock of transplanting, mist the plant regularly for several days. In dry climates, you can also place a small plastic tent over the plant to help keep humidity levels up. If you do this, keep your plant out of the sun, which could damage the plant by overheating it. Keep any newly transplanted bonsai shaded or otherwise out of direct light for several days to reduce transpiration of water from the leaves while your plant grows new hair roots. Your bonsai will have less ability to take in moisture until these roots have started to grow, and this needs to be balanced by reducing the amount of water lost through transpiration. Shading helps, but the main compensation here comes from removing much of the plant's foliage. Let's move on to this trimming

6

SHAPING YOUR FIELD-GROWN BONSAI

NOW THAT YOU'VE potted your field-grown bonsai, it is time to trim and shape it. This should be done immediately after potting. for several reasons. The most obvious reason is that you are just dying to see the shape of your bonsai emerge from what now looks like a potted bush. The most important reason is to reduce the transpiration of water to compensate for the plant's reduced ability to take up water due to root loss. And though it may be third in immediate importance, pruning to direct future growth is most important for the long-term benefit and beauty of your bonsai.

SELECTING THE MAIN BRANCHES
Begin the shaping process by placing the plant so that the base of the tree is close to eye level. You should be sitting comfortably and have the plant on a table or shelf where you can see it clearly while you work on it. Take some time to contemplate the current shape of the plant and consider the future growth and development of your bonsai. As you begin to decide which branches to leave and which to remove, keep in mind that branches can be wired to change the direction of their current and future growth. Before you are done, more than half of the foliage will be removed by thinning the branches and cutting back the tips of any branches that remain.

Examine the base of the trunk and the branches that sprout from it. Most healthy well-grown plants will be full and bushy, requiring more branches to be removed than will be

An English thyme plant freshly dug from the field after the growing season looks like a shapeless mass of foliage.

Remove the lower branches of the thyme to expose a shapely, curved trunk, and reduce the rootball to fit in a pot.

After potting the thyme, thin and trim the crown into a pleasing shape.

left on the tree. The first step is to decide which branches you will leave to form your bonsai. In a formal upright bonsai, the first main branch should be the thickest branch and be far enough up the main stem to allow definition of the trunk as the base of your bonsai. The second main branch should be slightly smaller in diameter than the first branch and should project to the opposite side of the trunk to balance the first branch. The third branch should be smaller yet and project to the back in order to provide depth to the bonsai.

That shape may not fit every plant with bonsai potential. Beautiful bonsai can be created that bear little resemblance to classic styles. Just as the sculptor sees and liberates his subject from a block of stone, the bonsai artist must see the bonsai inside the bush and carve away the extraneous material. But with this living sculpture, there is unlimited potential for future growth and shaping.

It may be difficult to decide which of the main branches to leave and which should be removed. If your plant is thick with small branches growing off the lower trunk and main branches, it will be difficult to see the main structure clearly. Before removing any of the large branches, clear that mess of little branches out of the way to make it easier to see the structure you have to work with. These undesirable branches should be trimmed flush to the stem, leaving no stub and causing as little scarring as possible. Start at the base of the trunk at ground level and move up the trunk, exposing the basic architecture of your bonsai as you work upwards, until you reach the zone of the crown of your bonsai. Be careful not to remove the little side branches too far out on the main branches at first. You don't want your bonsai to end up looking like a collection of pom-poms at the ends of the branches. Just expose enough of the trunk and main branches so that you can better determine which branches to leave and which to remove.

Formal bonsai rules require the removal of branches that cross each other or the main trunk. This is a good guideline to follow, although the occasional exception to this rule can sometimes create a unique bonsai with great appeal. Prostrate rosemary in particular often forms loops or other unusual shapes that can make striking bonsai.

Another rule of formal bonsai calls for all opposite branches to be removed; branches should alternate up the trunk, and side branches should alternate on the main limbs. Because of the opposite leaves and growth pattern of most herbs, many branches will have an opposite branch leaving the trunk or limb at the same position. One of these opposite branches should be removed. There should be very few exceptions to this rule, at least in the basic structure of the bonsai. It will be a rare bonsai that benefits from opposite branches. Unless your bonsai is grown in a cascade style, branches that grow in a downward direction or side branches that come off the bottom of main limbs should be removed.

This classic upright bonsai will be used in the following illustrations because its balance and flow represent principles that apply to the development of bonsai. Many herbal bonsai, however, will differ from this example.

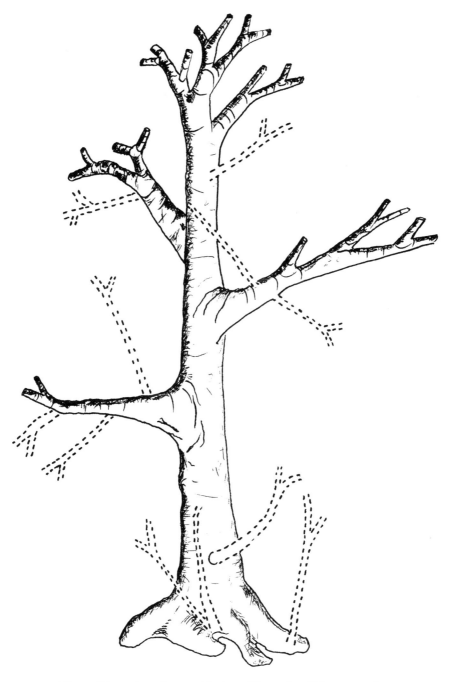

All small branches shown with dotted lines should be removed.

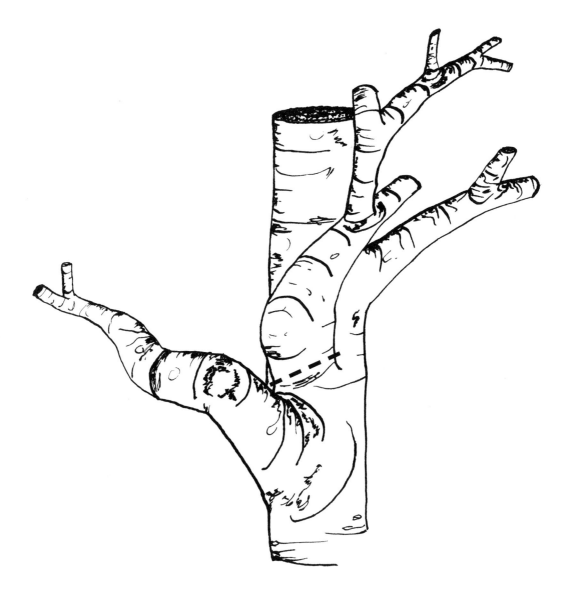

Remove branches that cross the trunk.

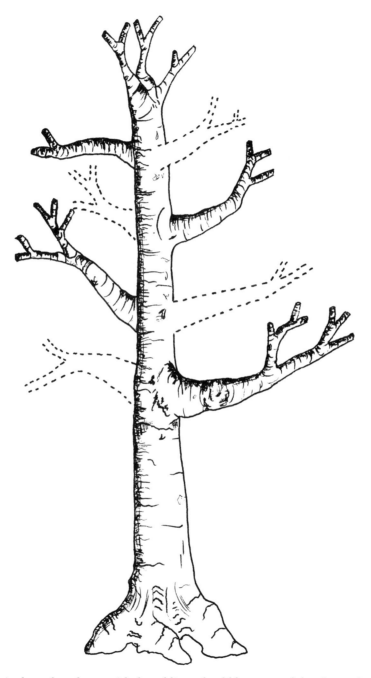

Opposite branches shown with dotted lines should be removed, leaving main branches that balance each side and provide depth.

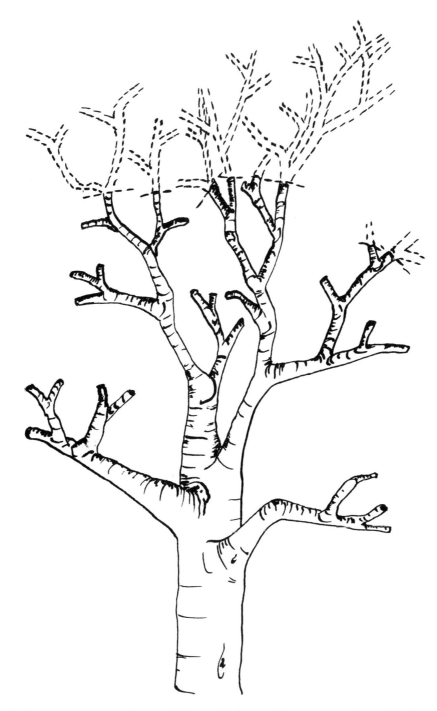

Medium-size branches shown with dotted lines should be pruned to fit within the crown.

These branches (tips removed for clarity) show the opposite growth pattern of most herb plants. Leave the branch that points in the direction of desired growth and remove the opposite twin.

This will leave the opposite branch that grows upward to define the direction of future growth for the bonsai. Herbs grow quickly, and branches that don't grow firmly upward can be pulled down by the weight of new growth on the tip of the branch.

SHAPING THE CROWN

At some point during the process of removing extra branches from the bottom up, it becomes possible to visualize the emerging crown of the bonsai. There are likely to be a number of long branches projecting well above the anticipated crown. Trim these back to fit within the emerging crown of the subject. Dramatic results can be obtained by cutting large branches severely back and allowing a new crown to grow around the stubs. An herbal bonsai trimmed from a large, thick bush can often have a nice crown and look good immediately. And with the faster growth of herbs, even a severely trimmed plant with large, bare stubs can develop a beautiful crown in a matter of months. In the long run (one or two years), the most dramatic bonsai will be created by severe initial pruning and the patience to wait for an entirely new crown to grow. Whether you take this long-range view or create an instant crown will depend on your desires and the amount of time that is available to you. I have pruned a beautiful "instant" bonsai out of a thick herbal bush in an afternoon in order to create a last-minute gift.

Depending on your plans for this bonsai, you should strike a balance between the instant gratification of leaving small green shoots on the trimmed branches to simulate a natural crown and your projection of the emerging crown from new growth after pruning. When you removed the small shoots from the trunk, forks, and main branches, you did not go too far out on the limbs at that time. Now continue this process and define the lower, inner edge of the crown. In order to achieve a good-looking bonsai with a suitable crown, it will be necessary to leave some small branches within a temporary crown that will be removed later after new growth occurs. These small branches that provide green foliage for the crown will be growing below secondary branches that will be left and developed during subsequent training.

When shaping main and side branches in the middle structure of your bonsai, the ideal branch would reflect the shape of the entire tree. The first side branch should be the largest, and branches should alternate to provide balance and fill out the crown. Side branches that project down from the bottom of main branches should always be removed. Remove enough side branches to allow the viewer to see into the tree, to appreciate the depth and internal structure of the bonsai. Side branches that obscure the view of the trunk and major branch forks should also be removed.

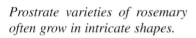
Prostrate varieties of rosemary often grow in intricate shapes.

Approximately five years old, this prostrate rosemary has been trained as a bonsai for only one month.

For a more ornate look, leave the open flowers when pruning prostrate rosemary.

Cuttings from bonsai can be rooted to start new plants.

Also about five years old, this prostrate rosemary has been planted in a deeper pot to help focus attention on the trunk and root structure.

Pruning reveals the interesting growth patterns of the trunk and branches of the bonsai.

This large, mutiple-trunk French lavender was planted in a deep, heavy pot to balance the size and weight of the crown, which is in full bloom.

Like the previous specimen, this single-trunk French lavender was carved from a two-gallon stock plant purchased at a nursery and has been in training for about a month.

Grown from a rooted cutting, this three-year-old variegated lemon geranium has been trained in an informal upright style, has never been field-planted, and spends its summers outside receiving a half-day of direct sun.

This three-year-old Costa Rican mint bush is growing in the slanting style. For balance, three pieces of petrified wood have been arranged to run parallel with the growth of the tree.

Choosing a different angle when displaying your bonsai can dramatically change its appearance.

Grown in a split-trunk style, this upright rosemary is about five years old, but its thick trunk and strong roots give the appearance of great age.

A close-up reveals the complex branch structure that can be achieved by using rosemary in bonsai.

Prune back the growing tips of all the branches left on the bonsai. This will define the outer boundary of the temporary crown as it grows to form the permanent crown that will continue to be developed for the life of your herbal bonsai. The exact placement of your cut will also determine where that branch forks and which direction the new branches will grow. Most herbs grow in an opposite pattern, with each succeeding leaf node growing leaves (and subsequent new shoots) rotated 90 degrees from the previous node. The strongest new growth will occur in the two shoots that are closest to the cut. Even if the shoots are not yet visible, you can count on a new shoot forming at the base of each leaf. The new shoot will grow in the direction that the leaf points.

SHAPING A CASCADE-STYLE BONSAI

When training a cascade-style bonsai, after the initial curve is created, most of the growth needs to be directed out and back up. The weight of the crown will continue to pull the tree down. Branches that grow straight down or from the underside of the trunk or main branches should usually be removed. Cascades should be kept thinned out more severely than upright bonsai to create a sparse appearance. Natural cascade trees are growing in a difficult environment and are spare and simple of line. A crown that is too large and heavy will look out of balance with the rest of the bonsai and the pot. A cascade bonsai should have an ethereal grace that contrasts to the massive pot—the "cliff"—that supports the base of the tree.

One variation on classic pure cascade style has a small branch projecting up and opposite to the growth of the trunk. This branch may come off the base of the trunk or may be a separate shoot that would technically make this a double-trunk bonsai. This upright growth should be kept small compared with the size of the main crown of the bonsai. Shape this growth like a tiny bonsai that reflects or provides contrast to the shape of the larger part of your cascade bonsai.

SHAPING A MULTIPLE-TRUNK BONSAI

Many herbs can be trained with multiple trunks. Preshaping a small herb to be field-grown with multiple trunks is easily done (see chapter 3). When acquiring plants that haven't been preshaped for bonsai, it is possible to find natural multiple-trunk herbs that will create beautiful bonsai. The multiple trunks are the main feature of this style of bonsai and should be emphasized. Classic form dictates a sparse, smaller crown that won't draw attention from the trunks. Certainly the crown of a three-trunk bonsai would have fewer branches and less foliage than three separate trees.

Cascade bonsai can be created with or without an upward projection. This can be a separate shoot or a low branch trained upward.

GREEN
BRANCH

WOODY
BRANCH

*To shape a woody branch, wrap wire around it in a spiral
fashion. For a thin green branch, use heavier wire and coil
it more loosely so that it serves as a brace.*

Multiple-trunk bonsai are often taller than other bonsai because the symmetry between long, bare trunks provides the dramatic effect of this style. The crown should begin farther from ground level than for any bonsai with a single trunk. Any main branches from one trunk that cross another trunk should be removed, allowing the viewer's gaze to follow the trunks up into the crown without distractions from crossing branches. The lowest branches should be on the outside of the outer trunks. Costa Rican mint bush often sends up multiple new strong shoots and is a good candidate for a multiple-trunk bonsai.

WIRING

The limber branches of herbs are ideal candidates for wiring. Extremely contorted shapes can be created from green branches that will turn woody and hard after the shape is formed. Wiring on traditional hardy bonsai trees often is left in place for years. With herbs, however, wire should be left in place for only three to nine months. Because of their fast growth rate, herbs will get scarred quickly if wrapped with wire. Observe your wired bonsai closely, looking for scarring several times per month. At the first evidence of scar formation, the wire must be removed. Remove wires by clipping them in several places and taking them out piece by piece. Trying to remove a long wire by unwrapping it in a single piece is difficult to do without damaging branches. If necessary, rewire the branch with a heavier wire in looser spirals to keep the desired shape.

Woody trees can be wired by wrapping the wire in spiral fashion around the branch. This can be carefully done with woody branches of herbs, keeping in mind that herbs grow quickly. Be careful to not wrap the wire too tightly, and watch very closely for scarring after the first three months. When wiring semigreen branches that are more limber, wiring technique must change. These are fast-growing parts of the plant and can easily be damaged by wire. They are also extremely flexible and can be looped or even carefully tied in loose knots. Use thicker wire, and use it as more of a brace than a coil. The wire still encircles the branch but in a much looser coil—as few as one to three wraps, where four to eight would be used on a woody branch. Two or three wraps may be strong enough to shape a 6-inch green branch. When the branch turns woody, it will hold its shape, and the wire can be removed. This should happen in several months.

Wiring techniques are featured and shown in detail in many bonsai books. Many people are intimidated by wiring, and this, along with other misperceptions about bonsai, keeps a lot of potential enthusiasts from ever attempting this fascinating art form. And countless bonsai have been scarred by first-time purchasers because the owner is so intimidated by the concept of wiring that wire already on the tree is not removed in time. I prefer a less structured, informal style where the bonsai is shaped with pruning alone and is seldom touched by wire. This provides a natural look that is quite realistic. Do whatever appeals to you, and work with the shapes your herb gives you.

7

TRAINING A CONTAINER-GROWN BONSAI

FIELD-GROWING AN HERB plant for an entire growing season is not necessary to produce an herbal bonsai. Many people don't have adequate garden space, and some of you may have elected to grow your young bonsai in large pots rather than in the field. Others may not wish to wait for spring plus a full growing season. A convenient alternative to field-growing your bonsai is to purchase a container-grown plant, although you won't have any control over the initial shaping of the young herb. Look for a frequently trimmed plant with lots of branching and a pleasing shape. (Chapter 3 gives advice on finding a good potential bonsai at your local nursery.)

Using container-grown plants, attractive bonsai can be created in an afternoon or shaped at a leisurely pace over several days. Natural root-growth habits in pots make it easier to expose gnarled roots that add character and apparent age. This is probably the easiest and certainly the quickest way to get started with herbal bonsai.

SHAPING THE BONSAI

It is best to shape the bonsai while still in the original pot. Handling a freshly repotted plant the way shaping requires can stress the plant too much if the roots are not settled enough to hold the plant steady. It is much easier on you and your herbal bonsai to take several hours or days to shape the top of the plant before root-pruning and repotting. You can even wait a couple days after shaping to root-prune and repot your bonsai.

This multiple-trunk, twisted bonsai was carved from a 2-gallon prostrate rosemary stock plant purchased at a nursery. The soil surface was decorated with creeping thyme, Irish moss, and amethyst crystals.

It can be hard to see the base of the trunk, especially if the soil level is low and the plant sits down in the pot. Slip the entire root ball out of the pot. This will make it easier to see the base of the trunk and to begin shaping your bonsai. Roots always grow downward, and even in very root-bound plants, the roots will circle the pot and continue to attempt growing down. There will often be an inch or two of soil on top of the main root ball that will have few if any roots. This can be removed to provide a taller trunk that will add stature to your bonsai. Exposing the trunk and base of your plant also will make it easier to shape your bonsai. Remove this soil carefully; avoid injuring the bark on the base of the trunk or on exposed old roots. Use your fingers or wooden tools rather than metal tools, which could easily damage your bonsai.

Underground trunk or roots usually appear whitish and lack the color of the exposed plant. They will darken up in a short time when exposed to the air and will soon look just like the rest of the trunk. Be careful not to expose fine hair roots to the air. A few of these can be removed from the newly exposed base of your bonsai. Don't prune or expose any roots at this time, except gnarled old roots that are right at the base of the trunk. Finish exposing and pruning these roots at the top of the root ball at the same time you prune the bottom of the root ball and repot your bonsai. When you are finished exposing the base of the trunk, place the plant back into its original pot. This will protect the roots and make less of a mess while pruning. You may wish to add some soil first to raise the ground level to the top of the pot. This will make it easier to see the lower trunk and branch structure while shaping your bonsai.

Prune your bonsai from the bottom up as described in chapter 6. With a purchased plant, it is not likely that you will have a plant capable of being trained in a formal style.

After shaping, the container-grown plant is ready to be potted.

This is no handicap unless you are determined to follow strictly classic rules. In that case, you should train a pot-grown plant from an early age. Some of the most attractive bonsai can come from older plants with unique shapes that might even directly contradict formal style. Take advantage of what the plant has to offer, whether or not it matches classic form. You can redirect the growth direction of woody branches with heavy wire.

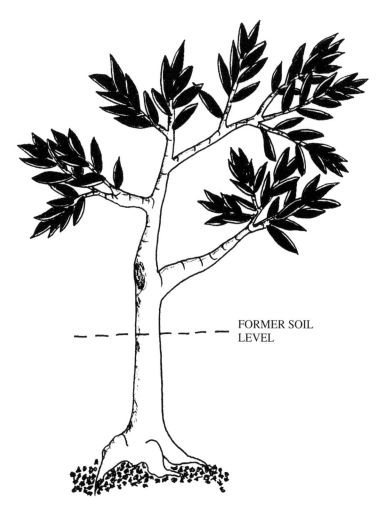

FORMER SOIL
LEVEL

The dirt above the root ball has been removed to expose the trunk.

ROOT-PRUNING

Repotting a container-grown plant requires severe root-pruning, especially on heavily root-bound plants. Large, gnarled roots can be exposed to form a unique base for a bonsai. Exposing roots is a similar process to shaping the branch structure. Large, well-shaped roots should be left and the smaller side roots removed. This is a slow process, and it may take several repottings and root-prunings to expose all the roots desired. Do not remove or expose too many roots at once. Remove fine hair roots from any large roots that will be exposed to the air above the new ground level. Because roots in containers grow down and around the inside of the pot, the new growth that reaches down into new soil at each repotting is the life support of the bonsai. Thus the older roots can be exposed without hurting the plant's ability to take in water and nutrients as they become more removed from the growing root tips. Another option at this stage is to place a rock under or between gnarled roots to develop the tree-over-rock style.

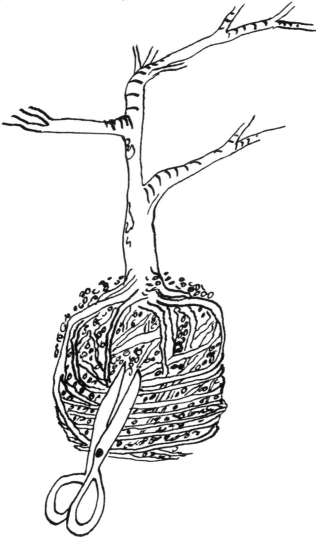

Trimmed and exposed, the plant is ready to root-prune.

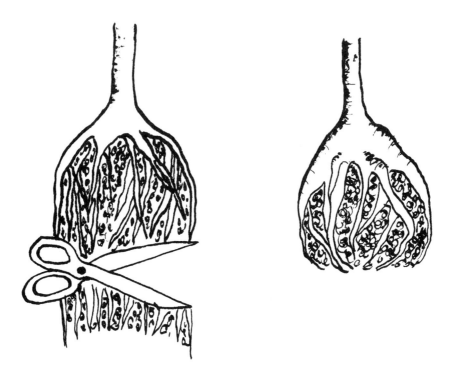

Pruning the roots will leave a compact root ball.

After exposing the basal root structure, the root tips need to be cut back to stimulate new root growth. Most large container-grown herbs will be very root-bound. When you slip the root ball out of the pot, you will see a mass of roots circling the bottom and sides of the pot. Most or all of these packed roots need to be trimmed off. Using a large knife or clippers, cut the bottom inch or two of roots off the root ball. If many packed roots remain encircling the root ball, trim these off as well. Fast-growing herbs will form well-packed roots like this very quickly in a good growing environment. As long as enough foliage is removed to balance the root loss, the root ball can and should be reduced in size by one-third to one-half. This will allow new roots to grow out into fresh soil in the next pot.

REPOTTING

You will probably move your bonsai into a pot smaller than the 1- or 2-gallon container it was growing in; it should certainly be shallower. A 5- to 8-inch clay or plastic pot makes a good intermediate home for your specimen. Round plastic bulb pans, used by commercial growers to force bulbs, are the best choice as an intermediate pot, especially if your desire

Carved from a one-gallon stock plant and root-pruned with a nursery shears, this large upright rosemary is ready to be planted in a bonsai pot.

The rosemary resembles a classic pine bonsai in the slanting style and was, therefore, planted in a standard brown, rectangular pot. The landscape around the rosemary, however, was decorated with agate and several ground covers to create a contrast to the traditional elements.

is to eventually place your bonsai into a shallow bonsai pot. These shallow pans help spread out the growth of the new root ball and shape it for life in a bonsai pot as shallow as 1 to 2 inches. After three to six months in the intermediate pot, it will be ready to repot into a bonsai container.

A large bonsai pot can often be used immediately with container-grown plants. You will need a pot at least 3 to 4 inches deep. The shape of the pot should be determined by your preferences and the shape and size of your bonsai.

Soil mixes are discussed in chapter 5. The only difference here is that it is less important to use local topsoil as part of your mix. A container plant will already be growing in a good soil mix similar to what you are using and doesn't need to adapt to the change from your local topsoil to a prepared mix.

Place screen over the drainage holes, and spread a layer of soil in the bottom of the pot. The depth of this layer is determined by the size of the root ball and the new soil level planned when exposing the base of your bonsai. This level should be located just above the top of the pot. This allows for proper viewing and gives a gentle slope for the soil from the bonsai's base to the sides of the pot. The soil level should be just below the rim at the walls of the pot, leaving just enough of a lip to keep soil from washing over the sides when watering. This level will vary depending on how you choose to finish off your bonsai—rocks, sand, gravel, moss, herbal ground covers, and figurines are among the possibilities (see chapter 9). Designing and creating a landscape that enhances your bonsai can be as important as your work on the bonsai itself. The larger pot used for herbal bonsai—especially when "carving" a large container plant—provides enough space to get very creative with landscaping.

Use root stimulators when watering in your freshly repotted bonsai. Herbal bonsai thrive in the brightest light but whenever repotted should be shaded for several days to reduce transpiration and allow new hair roots to grow. This will greatly reduce stress. In dry climates that typically have lots of bright sun, a freshly potted bonsai should be shaded or set back away from its bright window for up to a week before giving it that bright light that most herbs crave.

Even though herbs thrive in dry climates, they will use a lot of water. Most herbs like to dry out between waterings, but in a dry interior even a large pot can dry out in two or three days, especially if it has been in that pot for a while and is getting root-bound. The best way to water your bonsai is to immerse it in a pan, sink, or tub for ten to fifteen minutes to thoroughly wet the soil, and then allow it to drain before moving back to its place in the sun. When watering from above, it will take several pours to thoroughly wet the soil, especially if you used crystal polymers in your mix. Water can run through a pot too quickly to be fully absorbed. If your pot is sitting in a saucer or shallow tray, empty the tray after your first watering and water your bonsai again. With large pots, especially deep pots used for cascade bonsai, it takes more time to soak or more pours to be certain the soil is completely soaked.

8

CARING FOR YOUR HERBAL BONSAI

YOUR FIELD-GROWN HERBAL bonsai will have finished its dramatic growth phase by the time you dig it up and begin restricting its growth in a pot. If your plant has grown very large in the field, it will need to be planted in a 6- to 10-inch (1- to 2-gallon) intermediate pot for up to six months so that it will develop a more compact root ball that can be then reduced further to fit in a bonsai pot. Rosemaries in particular will benefit from an intermediate pot, but any herb that grows very large in the field should be planted in such a pot unless you have an extra-large bonsai pot. During this period, care will be much the same as if you put your herbal bonsai directly into a bonsai pot.

Your potted herbal bonsai will age slowly in a mature, slow-growing state that will not change dramatically unless you decide to put it through a field-growing condition again later in life. This can be done to revitalize an older plant that isn't growing well anymore or to induce dramatic new growth to change the shape of your bonsai. If you decide to do this, you will need to acclimate your bonsai to outside conditions again. Moving a plant directly from indoor conditions to full sun outside can be very damaging or even kill your plant. Give it a couple of hours of direct sun at first, and increase the amount of direct sun steadily over a period of several weeks before planting it into the field.

When your herbal bonsai is first potted up after its field-growing period, it will need special care. For the first two weeks after potting, keep it in a shaded spot away from direct sun. Until the plant develops new roots, transpiration must be reduced to prevent water loss and shock from damaging your herbal bonsai. The soil should be kept wet during this period, but you shouldn't need to water it too often. There is no well-developed root system to withdraw water from the soil, and by keeping your plant away from direct sun, bright light, and hot conditions, the soil will not dry out for several days. After the first week, move your bonsai into brighter light for a couple hours at a time, gradually increasing the amount of light to a full day. Watch your bonsai closely when you first move it into the sun. If the root system is not developed enough, your bonsai will start to wilt from lack of water in its vascular system. Move it back into the shade and it should recover. I have seen this particularly in rosemaries, which seem to need more time to grow new roots than other varieties of herbs. Your herbal bonsai will soon be ready to take its permanent location in a featured setting in your home.

LIGHT

The most important requirement for maintaining your herbal bonsai in a healthy, thriving condition is bright light. Herbs thrive in direct sun when planted in the garden and need bright light to maintain compact growth and look good. If you keep your herbal bonsai outside for part or all of the year, the ideal location is a spot where it will receive some direct sun during the morning but be shaded from the hot afternoon sun and protected from strong winds. Wind protection is especially important in dry climates, where harsh winds can dry out a plant even faster than the hot sun. Any plant in a pot will dry out faster than when planted in the ground. If your herbal bonsai has been moved from an intermediate pot to an even smaller bonsai pot, it will dry out more quickly and need daily watering except in the wettest climates.

Most herbal bonsai will be kept indoors part or all of the time. Today's growing interest in bonsai comes primarily from people who wish to keep bonsai as houseplants. Tender herb varieties such as rosemary, French lavender, lemon verbena, and others must be protected from killing frosts and thus must be kept indoors for long periods in most of North America. Since herbs do best in full sun, they need the brightest spot possible when grown indoors. A sunroom or solarium is the best choice and will keep your herbal bonsai looking its best. Though more homes today have solar areas, most people do not have this option yet. This means placing your herbal bonsai in front of a bright window. When not lit overhead by skylight or artificial light, herbs will grow strongly toward the window. Rotate the plant frequently to keep it growing evenly.

Herbs will survive in east, south, and west windows with some seasonal variation as to which window is best. Depth of roof overhangs and angles away from the appropriate cardinal direction will affect this; observe the sunlight in your home closely. West is generally better than east because the afternoon sun is more intense than morning sun. A northwest window will usually have less light than a southeast window, however, especially during winter. South-facing windows are usually your best choice, especially during the winter and in northern latitudes, where the sun gets quite low in the sky during fall and winter. Also in northern latitudes or where you have large overhangs, the summer sun will not provide direct sunlight through the window, and the east or preferably west windows will provide better light. In situations where you have less than optimal light during fall, winter, and spring, your herbal bonsai will benefit from spending time in bright outdoor light during the summer. Trim weak winter growth back rather severely before putting the plant outdoors. The new summer growth will be compact and attractive.

Lower-light conditions will result in weaker, elongated growth as your herbal bonsai stretches toward the light, and more frequent trimming will be required to keep your bonsai's shape. Observing such changes can help you decide whether a particular location is suitable. Artificial lighting can be used to supplement natural light or replace it entirely. It can be a great way to grow herbal bonsai and can be used in places where natural light is insufficient or absent. There are several types of lights that can be used. Full-spectrum bulbs are necessary to provide the frequencies and intensity required to keep your herbal bonsai thriving. Fluorescent tubes work well as far as growth is concerned, but there are some drawbacks to this type of lighting. Fluorescent fixtures are unattractive and difficult to disguise. Fluorescent lighting works best when positioned within 4 to 6 inches of the plant tops. This does not make for attractive display and works best when growing a group of plants that will be temporarily removed to be displayed elsewhere. This can be appropriate if you have a collection of bonsai and wish to display one or two at a time in a prominent position.

Some spotlight incandescent bulbs work very well. I use a 150-watt bulb extensively for both growing and display purposes. It provides a bright, natural-appearing light that supports great growth and looks good in a display situation. These bulbs are meant to be placed 5 to 6 feet away from the growing plants—far enough away from your herbal bonsai that the light won't distract the viewer. Smaller bulbs are also available, but all generate some heat and must be used only in porcelain sockets. One bulb illuminates an area about 1 yard square and therefore can be used to grow a group of herbal bonsai. Spotlight-type bulbs can be placed in a variety of attractive fixtures and can be recessed in some locations. These bulbs make it much easier to see and work on your herbal bonsai without having bright, distracting lights in your field of view.

You also can use lights to create artificial day-length periods to influence blooming patterns. Many herbs bloom naturally during mid to late summer and in response to longer days, which stimulate plants into bud production. Use an electric timer with adjustable on-off periods for setting day lengths to make this job easier. Restrict your trimming at this time, because buds form on growing tips that have attained some age. Your herbal bonsai will get a little lanky and look like it badly needs a haircut as it approaches flowering, but the flowers will make it worthwhile.

After flowering, trim your bonsai back to its proper shape. Shorten the day length again to allow the plant to rest between flowering periods. Always adjust the day length gradually, no more than an hour at a time, and give each change a week or so to allow your herbal bonsai to acclimate to the new conditions. Longer day lengths stimulate faster flowering, so don't be afraid to work up to eighteen hours of light and then back to ten or twelve hours for resting.

Scented geraniums need to be slightly pot-bound in order to bloom. When repotted in late summer or early fall and then left untrimmed, they will bloom throughout the winter if given bright enough light. Geraniums have beautiful flowers and are well worth the effort it takes to bring them into bloom during the off-season. They will bloom better if kept a little on the dry side during the blooming period.

TEMPERATURE

Most plants, including herbs, perform better when night temperatures are 10 to 15 degrees F. (5 to 10 degrees C.) cooler than day temperatures. During the winter, lowering your thermostat at night will benefit your herbal bonsai as well as conserve energy and save you money on your heating bill. Modern centrally heated homes still have microclimates where the temperatures can vary quite a bit. Certain rooms or even spots within rooms can be cooler or warmer than the setting on your thermostat. In a well-ventilated house, the temperature can vary greatly at different heights within the room. Cool air is heavy, and the temperature near the floor can easily be 10 to 15 degrees F. (5 to 10 degrees C.) cooler than a thermostat set at eye level. If you have a deep windowsill, you can set your herbal bonsai behind heavy drapes that are closed at night to provide cooler night temperatures. Keep the locations of heater ducts and air-conditioning vents in mind, and use a thermometer that measures daily maximum and minimum temperature to fine-tune the location of your home's microclimates. Nearby windows can be opened at night when outdoor temperatures are appropriate to cool off your herbal bonsai.

WATER

Water is also an important factor when considering long-term care of your herbal bonsai. The moisture needs of your herbal bonsai will vary according to season, location, length of time since last repotting, and crown size. Longer periods of daylight will stimulate plants to use more water, and intense sunlight or hot spotlights will also cause plants to dry out more quickly. Compound these conditions with a root-bound plant, and your herbal bonsai can get dangerously dry in just a day or two. Your herbal bonsai will need more water in the summer than during the winter, and an herbal bonsai sitting in a south or west window will dry out faster than one in an east window.

When your herbal bonsai is first repotted, it won't dry out as quickly as it will when its roots fill the pot. Although direct drying action on the dirt is a significant factor, most water is lost by transpiration through the plant's foliage. When the roots fill the pot, they will more quickly remove water from the soil. And by the time the roots have grown this much, the crown also will have grown and will transpire more water. Even if your herbal bonsai has been trimmed regularly, the crown will be thicker and have more foliage. A heavy pruning will reduce the plant's ability to transpire water for a while. This is why pruning is always recommended when transplanting or root-pruning.

Outdoors, an herbal bonsai will need watering every day to once every three days, depending on the weather and the other factors discussed. Indoors, an herbal bonsai in good shape should need watering once every three to four days. When an indoor herbal bonsai starts drying out too quickly, it is time to repot it.

When watering your herbal bonsai, it needs to be soaked thoroughly rather than just giving it a little drink. The traditional way to water bonsai is to immerse the pot in a tub of water until it stops bubbling and the soil is thoroughly soaked. Although this is probably the best method, it is not necessary. If you prefer to water your bonsai by pouring the water on the soil surface, it will take several repeated waterings to soak the soil thoroughly. Especially with a plant that has been in the same pot for a while, water develops channels that allow it to run right through a pot without soaking the soil. In this case, the bonsai must be watered repeatedly to soak the soil. Move your herbal bonsai to the sink or a tub (outside if the weather is nice) for watering, and allow it to drain before placing it back on display in your home.

FERTILIZER

Traditional bonsdai varieties such as pines, junipers, or maples are fertilized once or twice a year, with the fertilizer mixed at about half strength. Herbal bonsai are fast growing compared with traditional bonsai and need to be fertilized more like houseplants. You do not want to stimulate excessive growth in your herbal bonsai, however, except during the field-growing period. Weaker organic fertilizers like fish emulsion or manure tea can be used on a regular basis several times per month. Fertilize more often during the summer or any warm, long day-length periods and less often or at lower concentrations during the winter, especially when your herbal bonsai is in a low-light situation. Stronger commercial fertilizers such as a 20–20–20 water-soluble all-purpose blend should be used no more than once a month.

Another method that is less troublesome than regularly mixing chemicals or having your house reek of rotted fish is using time-release fertilizer pellets that are mixed into the soil. These last from six to eighteen months, although that will vary depending on how much you water your herbal bonsai. Watering releases the fertilizers, and periods of frequent watering, indicative of faster growth conditions, will cause the plant food to be released more quickly. Other water-soluble fertilizers can be used to supplement if needed when the herbal bonsai has been in the same pot for a long time. A blossom-stimulating fertilizer such as 10–30–20 or 12–36–14 can be used, especially in conjunction with day-length periods, to stimulate flower production.

TRIMMING

Traditional bonsai are usually pruned once or twice a year. This is appropriate for slow-growing tree species, but as herbal bonsai is fast growing, it will need regular trimming to maintain an attractive, compact appearance. Once the crown is developed, this trimming will resemble a light haircut more than anything else and may need to be done as much as once or twice a month. Frequent light trimmings maintain the tightest growth and most compact crown. Branching occurs each time the tips are trimmed, and if the new growth isn't trimmed close to the previous cut, the crown will get lanky and begin to look bedraggled.

There are a couple of exceptions to the frequent trimmings your herbal bonsai requires during normal care. When you plan to repot your bonsai, skip the last couple of trims so that there will be plenty of foliage to remove after repotting. This heavier trim will reduce the plant's ability to transpire water and compensate for the plant's reduced ability to take up water after the roots are trimmed. Most herbal bonsai should be repotted once a year. If your bonsai shows signs of stress from drying too rapidly and gets quite root-bound, you will have to repot more often. Using a larger pot will allow more time to pass between repottings. Most herbs can be repotted several times per year without harm if so desired. When repotting a mature herbal bonsai, use the same soils and techniques discussed in chapter 7 for potting a container-grown plant.

Avoid trimming the growing tips when attempting to bring your herbal bonsai into flower. Buds develop on the very tips of long branches in some varieties, such as French

Slow-growing shrubs, such as this variegated sweet myrtle, may only need to be trimmed two or three times a year. This five-year-old bonsai looks a little wild after six months without a trim.

lavender and lemon verbena, and on lateral buds near the growing tips in others, such as rosemary. In either case, the tips are not trimmed for two to four months and can get rather long and wild. When the flowers begin to fade, cut these tips back and resume frequent trimmings while the plant rests from its blooming phase. This trim can be a good time to repot your plant if needed or desired.

Another characteristic of herbs is their tendency to sprout new green shoots from even the lower woody sections of the trunk. These shoots can be either small and weak or sometimes the strongest shoot on the entire plant. These shoots should be removed as soon as they show in order to keep your bonsai's neat appearance. Costa Rican mint bush sends out

Remove the shoots that grow downward to reveal the lower branches, and trim the higher shoots to form the crown.

strong shoots that can be quickly trained as new branches or trunks. This can add to or dramatically change the shape of your bonsai. Tired old foliage can be cut back to stubs as new shoots are trained into a crown and the base of your bonsai thickens with age into a gnarly, old stump. Scented geraniums are very shallow rooted, and repeated waterings will often wash the roots clean and leave them exposed to the air. New shoots often grow from these exposed roots and look like new plants sprouting out of the ground. These should be removed as they appear. If a section of root is left attached, it can be potted right up. Scented geraniums are known for throwing sports, or mutations that lead to new varieties. These new shoots growing from the roots are the best place to look for these variations.

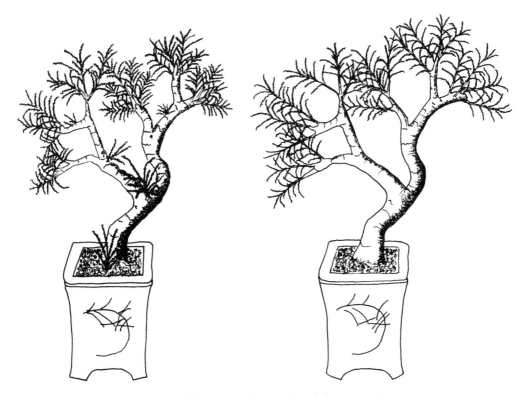

Remove new shoots from the trunk and the exposed roots.

PEST CONTROL

A problem you will run into sooner or later is pest control. Watch for bugs when bringing plants into the house or moving plants outside and then back in. Insects are also brought home by brushing against infected plants at nurseries or even a friend's house and carrying them home on your clothes. Although some herbs seem to never be bothered by insects, other varieties are attractive to several common house and garden pests. The fragrant lemon verbena and Costa Rican mint bush are virtual pest magnets. Aphids will attack almost anything, spider mites like rosemary, and white flies will attack many varieties, their favorites being geraniums, lemon verbena, and Costa Rican mint bush.

With any herb that you plan to consume, it is important to use nontoxic methods of control. If you have just a few small specimens, cleaning your herbal bonsai by hand and with sprays of water is feasible. White flies can be easily controlled by hand. Check the undersides of the leaves for larvae. For heavier infestations, you may need to pluck off some

The crown can be developed further by cultivating a stong new shoot, as in this two-year-old Costa Rican mint bush.

leaves if they show colonies of larvae. Mealybugs should also be controlled by hand and water, paying close attention to branch joints and leaf axils, where mealies lay their eggs in cottony masses. Aphids can be controlled by hand or washed off with directed sprays of water. Spider mites are harder to see and control but can be washed off with strongly directed sprays of water. The next step would be to use a soapy spray, which is safe enough if trimmings are washed before using. For a bad infestation on a valuable specimen, you may decide to use more toxic pesticides to save the plant at the cost of using it herbally.

Rosemaries are subject to powdery mildew, which appears as a fuzzy grayish white covering on the leaves. This is especially likely during the winter. Low light, lack of air flow, and large fluctuations in daily temperatures promote growth of this fungus. The best way to control this is by changing these conditions. The easiest way is to use bright, hot, full-spectrum spotlights, especially overnight when cool temperature extremes occur.

Changing the plant's location or using a fan to circulate air also can solve this problem. Persistent cases can be treated with commercial fungicides, which are quite effective but can't be employed if you wish to use your herbal bonsai trimmings in cooking.

As you care for your herbal bonsai over the months and years, be observant of the plant's condition and its responses to changes that occur throughout the year naturally or those that you effect to achieve different results. As you live with your herbal bonsai, you will continue to learn new ways to train bonsai and discover novel uses for your herbs.

9

DRESSING UP YOUR BONSAI

BONSAI CAN BE grown in many different types of pots. An herbal bonsai-in-training that has just been dug from the field will do best in an intermediate pot such as a 1- or 2-gallon nursery pot for the first six months or so. Eventually you will wish to display your herbal bonsai in a more attractive setting. Classic bonsai pottery is the obvious choice. There are hundreds of styles, sizes, and colors available. Most retail centers can stock only a small selection of what is available. If you want something specific or unusual, you may need to look around at a number of shops. If you can't find what you want, talk to the salesperson or manager about your needs. Dozens of wholesale suppliers publish catalogs showing their wares, and a good retailer will help you find what you desire. Retail bonsai advertisers in gardening magazines also offer a large selection.

The size and shape of the pottery are extremely important in the overall appearance of your bonsai. Tradition calls for a pot whose length is two-thirds to three-fourths the height of the tree and whose width is one-half the height. The ideal depth of the pot traditionally is equal to the diameter of the trunk. The fast-growing roots and heavier water requirements of herbal bonsai may preclude using a pot this shallow, however. Your herbal bonsai will be easier to care for in a deeper pot. Scented geraniums and Costa Rican mint bushes in particular seem to dry out quickly and will be better off in a pot deeper than tradition calls for. The deepest pots are used for for cascade and semicascade bonsai, partly to offset the hanging weight of the tree and its foliage.

The shape of the pot suggests the terrain in which the bonsai grows. Tall pots represent cliffs—the natural terrain of a cascade tree growing out and down from a high precipice. Shallow pots suggest plains and meadows and should be used for group plantings and when you wish to give some emphasis to the surrounding landscape. Round pots suggest a soft beauty and are suited for upright bonsai with soft, round crown shapes. Flowering plants also look good in round pots, which have the advantage of being viewable from all angles. Oval pots resemble the curves found in riverside and lakeside scenes. Rectangular pots are blocky and angular, with a distinct front, and represent mountains or other rough terrain. Think about the shape of your bonsai and the type of terrain that would produce that shape in the wild. A pot should be matched to the style of the individual bonsai.

The color of the pot is also important. Traditional philosophy recommends plain, unglazed pots in muted shades of red, gray, or brown for coniferous trees like pines and junipers. These shades are most appropriate for an herb that has a strong resemblance to these trees, such as rosemary. Brighter, glazed colors should be used for flowering, fruiting or variegated bonsai. The most vibrant colors should be reserved for miniature bonsai. A fancy porcelain pot with a painted scene or striking pattern would look out of place displayed outside with traditional bonsai, but the very same pot planted with an appropriate free-form herbal bonsai can make a spectacular indoor decoration. Fine cracks in the glaze, known as crazing, mute the color somewhat and help create a feeling of great age. Different colors have connotations that can add to the overall effect of your herbal bonsai. Blue is associated with water. Green implies lush summer growth, and yellow and shades of red and brown suggest fall. Ivory, black, and brighter shades of red express the characteristics of rocks and mountains. Relate the color of the pot to the imagined home of your herbal bonsai. You may wish to choose a particular color to match the decor in your home or just because you like the shade. A display of a collection of herbal bonsai will look better with a variety of pottery colors.

The only drawback to classic bonsai pottery is the high price, especially as you get into the larger sizes. Most of this pottery is imported from China or Japan, and there can be wide variation in quality and price. Herbal bonsai need to be repotted more frequently than traditional varieties and can be transplanted rather often to suit your needs and desires. It helps to have a large selection of pots available to choose from, and there are less expensive alternatives that can look quite good. Plastic bonsai pots can be found not only in the commonly seen brown, rectangular style but also in round, octagonal, and tall vase (for cascades) shapes in other colors, some with quite attractive glossy finishes. These are more expensive than plastic greenhouse pots but are inexpensive compared with fine pottery.

Lemon verbena is a large, fast growing shrub that should be planted in a deep pot to provide room for growth and to balance the heavy crown.

Unless you are growing a cascade-style bonsai, use a shallow pot. This will help train a shallow root ball and keep your herbal bonsai from being dominated by its pot. Azalea pots, which are shorter than standard pots, are a good place to start, especially for intermediate phases. It can take several repottings to train a field-grown root ball to the shape of a pot as shallow as 1 1/2 to 3 inches. Bulb pans are shallower than azalea pots and work even better. Clay saucers can be converted into effective shallow pots by using a masonry drill bit to drill drainage holes in the bottom. Planting a small grove of three or five herbs in a large saucer of 16 to 18 inches can create a stunning landscape. Keep your eyes open and you will find many different containers that can be converted into bonsai pots. Good drainage is a must, and a masonry drill bit can be a big help. Another option is to make your own pottery. If you have no experience or access to a kiln, take a class and tell your instructor what you wish to do. Look at universities, adult continuing education programs, art-supply stores, or city recreation programs to find a class that will suit your needs. It can be very satisfying to create your herbal bonsai from the pot up.

SAND OR GRAVEL

Large herbal bonsai require a big pot, and there can be a large area of exposed soil on the surface. Moss and sand are used in traditional bonsai to give a natural appearance, but the problem with moss is that it won't survive as a houseplant. Perhaps the easiest and most trouble-free way to cover the soil is with sand or small gravel chips. Most sand and gravel companies have a variety of natural rock blends and for a nominal fee will let you fill a couple of buckets with a lifetime supply of various bonsai gravels. This will give you a simple, low-maintenance ground covering that won't distract the viewer's attention from the bonsai. Some bonsai look best with this style of ground cover. If you can't resist decorating your bonsai with rocks, plants, or figurines, you will still need some sand or gravel to fill in the spaces. Fine white sand can be used to suggest water, as the Japanese have done for centuries. Your herbal bonsai can be landscaped with several ground-cover plants using white sand to represent a small stream running beneath the tree.

ROCKS

There are several ways to use rocks to enhance the appearance of your bonsai. The traditional approach involves using weatherworn rock, possibly lichen encrusted, to fashion a natural landscape appearance around the base of your bonsai. Look closely at the surface texture and directional lines of flow of your rock specimens. Angular, blocky pieces of rock should be used with strong bonsai that have sharp angles in the branches or crown. A tall rock with vertical striations will reflect the shape of a long, straight trunk without branches on the side of the tree next to the rock. A softly curving bonsai with billowing mounds of foliage should be matched with rocks that have rounded shapes. Ground-cover plants and sand or gravel should be used in combination with the rocks to fashion an appropriate landscape.

When placing rocks around your bonsai, try to create the appearance of a natural wild landscape, where features are at random. Your bonsai should not look like a formal garden where everything is placed equidistant in straight rows. Look at your rock placement from all angles, including from directly above, to make sure they are not in too regular a

Rocks and gemstones can be used in bonsai to create miniature landscapes. Rose quartz, elbaite tourmaline, and aquamarine beryl crystals add scenic texture to this sweet myrtle grove.

formation. Always use an odd number of objects. When dealing with small numbers, it is much easier to arrange an odd number of objects in a random appearance. An even number of objects always seems to look too regular to be natural.

Another approach is to use specimens of crystals, semiprecious gemstones, or fossils that are as interesting on their own as the bonsai specimen itself. Many people feel this looks too artificial and can distract the viewer from the bonsai. They have a point, but with taste and some restraint, you can create a stunning landscape that will enhance an already spectacular herbal bonsai. Differences in scale between leaf size and crystal or fossil size can be a big factor. Small specimens can make an attractive representation of a deposit in a natural setting. Use a sprinkling of tiny crystals or a sedimentary rock encrusted with small fossils to keep the appearance in scale with your bonsai, and some striking results will occur.

Petrified wood is a semiprecious gemstone that can form as perfect limb casts and show wood grain or bark even in small pieces. Nice specimens will give the appearance of a fallen, possibly half-rotted tree trunk lying in the forest. Several pieces might be placed in a straight line to suggest a fallen trunk.

A large piece of agate representing a cliff provides balance to this cascade prostrate rosemary.

There are other ways to work semiprecious stones into your landscaping. There are many varieties of agate that have bands and swirls of every color imaginable. Agate can be found in nearly every state, and the play of colors can resemble the sedimentary bands seen in such places as the Grand Canyon and many other beautiful areas. A massive chunk of bright pink rose quartz can be reminiscent of a cliff face in the Black Hills of South Dakota. Rock studded with garnets can be found in the Black Hills and many other areas. A flat sheet of mica crystals or even mica schist can be used to represent a sparkling lake surrounded by mounds of green ground cover to suggest hills. Massive pieces of many kinds of rock can be placed at the back of a large pot to give the appearance of mountains in the distance.

A traditional method of using rocks in bonsai is the root-over-rock arrangement. This involves washing the soil off the roots of your bonsai and selecting an appropriate rock to wrap the roots around before planting in a deep pot. Most of the rock will be buried as your bonsai develops new roots that grow downward in the soil. More of the rock becomes exposed with successive repottings, and you must remove the fine side roots from the larger exposed ones. After several repottings, most of the rock will be visible and your root-over-rock bonsai will be ready to display in a bonsai pot. This process can be accelerated by field-planting your prebonsai with its roots already wrapped around a rock; however, you will need to shade it from the sun for several days while the roots recover and start to grow into the new soil.

The best rocks to use for root-over-rock are those that have lots of cracks and crevices for the roots to cling to. Quite massive rocks can be used to create the appearance of a tree perched upon a large boulder or even the edge of a cliff. Fine-grained common rocks, such as granite, limestone, or volcanic tuffa, will create the most natural appearance.

Beautiful rock specimens can be collected all over the country. Whether walking in your local woods or taking the trip of a lifetime, keep your eyes open for attractive rocks. Many state and regional guidebooks are available that provide maps and list hundreds of collecting locations. Stop at rock shops when traveling to find these guidebooks, and ask plenty of questions. You can see what is available locally, as well as rocks from all over the world, and can obtain some beautiful material inexpensively.

Before collecting rocks, make certain it is legal and permissible to do so. It is illegal to collect rocks in national, state, and local parks, although most national forest and Bureau of Land Management land is open to private collectors for personal use. Get the owner's permission before you collect on private land.

Both the Chinese and Japanese have developed styles of rock planting that are related to and displayed with bonsai. These plantings can be created of rocks alone or in combination with sand, gravel, soil, water, plants, and figurines to create landscapes that represent wilderness scenes or natural areas showing human influences (see chapter 10). Using rocks to decorate your herbal bonsai is a way of combining rock planting with bonsai. The bonsai may remain the center of focus, with the landscape complementing the bonsai rather than dominating the scene, or a small herbal bonsai can be used to accent a large rock planting where the landscape is the central focus.

GROUND COVERS

Using plants as a ground cover for your herbal bonsai adds a whole new dimension to the art form. The natural aged trees that bonsai represent are found in landscapes filled with rocks and plants. Artfully placed ground covers can enhance a bonsai and draw the viewer in. Many ground covers bloom with delicate little flowers that can look like spring wildflowers in full bloom on the forest floor. It takes a little time and trouble, but fields of flowers under your bonsai in a tastefully arranged landscape are well worth it. Using a larger pot or a drilled clay saucer with a large surface area will give you enough space to arrange rocks and several ground-cover plants in a beautiful landscape that will add dimension to your herbal bonsai.

The ground covers will need dividing and replanting several times a year. Because herbal bonsai can be repotted frequently and tolerate root disturbance, ground covers can be changed, divided, and replanted as often as desired. Most of the ground covers are perennials that do best in full sun and may slowly deteriorate or develop tall, weak growth in lower-light situations. They can be clipped like grass, allowed to hang over the edge of the pot, or given supplemental light. Artificial lights also allow you to control light periods and bring the ground cover into bloom when desired. For shows or to use your herbal bonsai as a centerpiece, you can plant fresh ground covers that are already in bloom. Fresh ground covers can be purchased inexpensively at your local nursery, or you can grow a selection to use when needed. These plants are shallow rooted and will dry out faster than your herbal bonsai, requiring more frequent waterings. They will wilt before the bonsai and can be used as an indicator to tell you when to water.

There are a number of plants that work well as ground covers. Don't be afraid to experiment with varieties that aren't mentioned here; countless plants can be adapted for this use. Different species may survive better in your geographical area and your herbal bonsai's particular location in your home. Even a variety that doesn't survive well for you may be worth using for the short term to create a particular effect for a special occasion. You can dress your herbal bonsai in a landscape of many colors. Scale will again be your main concern.

There are a couple of houseplant varieties that will grow well in low light. **Baby's tears** (*Helxine soleirolia*) is a common, tiny-leaved plant sold in greenhouses all over the country. It can form a dense, green mat of foliage that looks lush and tropical. It grows so well it is considered a weed in some warmer areas and where it escapes in greenhouses. It needs to be kept a little wetter than most of the other varieties, so you will need to water more often. There are both green and golden forms of this plant.

Creeping charlie (*Pilea depressa*) is a little larger in stature than baby's tears and works well with larger bonsai or when used to represent shrubby foliage a little taller than a ground cover. It roots so easily that you can just pinch a small tip or two, strip some lower leaves, and plant it directly in your landscape. As it grows, it will need regular pinching to keep it compact and under control, or you can let it hang 6 inches over the edge of the pot. If it gets too big, just pull it out and replant a piece of it. There is a variegated variety of this species that looks dramatic against the greens of other ground covers and your herbal bonsai.

If you can find one of the tiny-leaved variations of **English ivy** (*Hedera helix*), you can add even more texture to your landscape. Single stems can look like a vine and be arranged to climb the trunk or hang over a rock or any another feature in the landscape. Ivy can also be grown as a bushy little plant with short stems to represent a shrub or small bush in your landscape. This effect looks quite good with a large herbal bonsai. Fresh cuttings of ivy are very hardy and will usually root, with the help of a little rooting hormone, when planted directly in place in your pot.

Corsican mint (*Mentha requienii*) has a strong mint scent that gives it another common name, creme-de-menthe plant. This tiny mint, which resembles baby's tears, forms tight mats less than 1 inch tall and stays shorter than most other ground covers. It needs to be kept a little on the moist side and can be temperamental in some locations. Tiny lavender flowers form in the summer and can be induced creating a long-day photoperiod with artificial lighting.

Several species of **thyme** (*Thymus* spp.) work well as bonsai ground covers, and they can bloom quite freely in response to long days. Caraway thyme (*Thymus herba-barona*) has a distinct caraway odor and reaches 2 to 5 inches tall. Its pink flowers are striking against its dark green foliage. Its graceful, airy appearance and tiny leaves can resemble a forest. Old specimens of this species can be used to create miniature bonsai just a few inches tall.

Woolly thyme (*T. pseudolanuginosus*) has fuzzy, silver-gray foliage that contrasts well with other ground covers. It is low growing (less than $1/2$ inch tall) and occasionally shows pink flowers. This variety works well as a bonsai ground cover, and its distinctive foliage makes it an important component in a collection of ground covers. Let it get a little dry before watering.

Creeping thyme (*Thymus* spp.) is a good ground cover that comes in several species and many varieties. There is much confusion in the names of creeping thymes sold at garden centers, and there are a lot of misnamed varieties out there. Pay more attention to the appearance and growth habits of prospective ground covers than their listed names. Mother of thyme (*T. praecox*) is very common and has purple flowers, although it can get a little tall for smaller bonsai. The next three varieties are probably *T. praecox* but will most likely be named as varieties of *T. serpyllum*. 'Coccineum' has bright scarlet flowers, 'Alba' has white ones, and 'Nutmeg' also has white flowers as well as a delightful fragrance. Miniature creeping thyme (*T. serpyllum* 'Minus') is perhaps the best variety to use. Its soft, green foliage has short internodes, which give it a congested appearance, and it forms thick mats less than 1 inch in height. 'Minus' is the most dwarfed form of creeping thyme and survives better than other varieties when grown as a houseplant. Though not as floriferous as other thymes, it will bloom with tiny white flowers in response to long days.

This multiple-trunk English thyme has tall Irish moss in bloom that will need to be trimmed after flowering to display the lower trunks of the bonsai.

Pearlwort is a very attractive plant with two varieties appropriate for bonsai. Irish moss (*Sagina subulata*) has deep green, dense, mosslike foliage that resembles a green lawn with perfect scale for even the smallest bonsai. Scotch moss (*S. subulata* 'Aurea') is a golden form of the same plant. Both of these varieties make great landscape plants for your herbal bonsai and flower easily. Their tiny, white flowers have yellow stamens and resemble Shasta daisies scattered across a lawn. With bright enough light, these plants will stay well under 1 inch tall. They can grow to 3 inches tall with a sparse appearance in low light but respond well to trimming. Look closely before "mowing," however, as flowers can form even on sparse tips, and you want to wait until after the blooming period.

Stonecrops (*Sedum* spp.) are another group with a lot of potential for bonsai ground covers. They need to dry out between waterings and do best in brighter light. Stonecrops come in many sizes and have solid-colored or variegated foliage in colors ranging from bright greens through shades of blue, gray, pink, red, purple, and white. Flowers will bloom anytime from midsummer until late fall for different varieties under normal conditions. Blossom colors include white, pink, rose, blue, red, and yellow. There are possibly six hundred species and countless varieties in this genus, which makes for undeniable confusion over their names. As with the creeping thymes, pay more attention to the appearance and growth habits of available varieties than to their names. Look for small, low-growing varieties that will be in scale with your herbal bonsai. The two best varieties, which do well indoors, are miniature sedum (*S. requieni*) and tear-drop sedum (S. sp. 'Baby Tears'). The miniature variety forms a dense mat of tiny green leaves under $1/2$ inch tall with white flowers. Other common stonecrops include, *S. acre, S. album, S. album* 'Blue Ridge,' *S. brevifolium,* and *S. spurium* ('Dragon's Blood').

Scabplant (*Raoulia australis*) is a fine-textured silver creeper that resembles lichen. It needs dry conditions and is temperamental indoors but has a dramatic appearance and is especially worth using for short periods for display or a photo session.

Several varieties of **speedwell** (*Veronica* spp.) can be used as permanent ground covers or can be planted temporarily for their delicate flowers. Woolly veronica (*V. pectinata*) and creeping speedwell (*V. repens*) form low-growing mats to 2 or 3 inches, with flowers shading from white to pink with touches of blue and lavender. Taller varieties like *V. alliona, V. filaformis,* and *V. liwanensis* flower in shades of blue and can be used as a ground cover with taller bonsai or to create a small shrub in the landscape of a shorter herbal bonsai.

FIGURINES

Clay miniatures are one more way you can decorate your herbal bonsai. Figurines include people in poses borrowed from traditional Chinese paintings: Activities from solitary meditation to scholarly debate to fishing, drinking, or riding animals have been depicted. Other miniatures include animals such as turtles, cranes, water buffalo, and elephants, as well as boats, bridges, pavilions, and buildings from thatched huts to pagodas. Figurines are available in many sizes, ranging from less than $1/2$ inch to more than 4 inches. A single piece can make a nice statement and relate the bonsai to other aspects of life. A clutter of figurines will detract from your specimen, however. An herbal bonsai should look like a wild tree, not a yard specimen belonging to someone with a fondness for collecting lawn ornaments, so keep it simple.

There are many ways to accent and decorate the landscape around an herbal bonsai Don't limit yourself to a single style or vision. The same type of landscape when repeated on an entire collection becomes boring and won't properly reflect the individual character of each bonsai. If you use figurines, don't create an entire scene on each specimen. Use a single figure on some to provide contrast to busy scenes on others, and leave one or two bonsai without any figurines for a completely natural appearance. Always be on the lookout for new varieties of plants and other appropriate materials to enhance your bonsai. Traditional bonsai has an austere appearance, using just sand and moss to avoid drawing attention from the bonsai. Art grows by stretching the boundaries of tradition, so be creative and put as much work into the landscape as you do the herbal bonsai itself. You'll be pleased with the results.

10

DISPLAYING HERBAL BONSAI

HERBAL BONSAI OFFER unique opportunities for display and use that expand upon traditional ideas. Many basics of display will be the same as with classic bonsai, although the special characteristics of herbs will suggest some changes.

THE DISPLAY AREA

The location where you might wish to display your herbal bonsai is probably not the best place to grow it. Herbs need bright light to look their best, and that bright window, sun-room, or greenhouse where your bonsai lives just won't show it off to its best advantage. Traditional bonsai are grown outdoors or in greenhouses and are brought indoors only for short periods to display them. A permanent display will have bonsai rotated in and then back out to the growing area as it is replaced with another bonsai out of the collection. This can be done with herbal bonsai, although they will tolerate the conditions in a less-than-adequate display area for a longer period of time than the traditional bonsai species. The limiting factor here is lack of light, and this can be remedied by using a spot grow light. This will keep your herbal bonsai looking its best and even allow you to grow it full-time in the display area if desired.

A spectacular herbal bonsai deserves to be displayed in a special setting that draws attention and provides the proper atmosphere to set the mood. A display area should be planned and set up in an appropriate place in your home. The Japanese have a tradition of setting up a recessed display area, known as the *tokonoma,* just inside the main entryway of the house. You can create a similar setting without an architecturally recessed alcove by placing a shelf, table, or stand in front of a plain wall. The formal *tokonoma* consists of a hanging scroll, a bonsai, and an accent. This accent can be a companion planting, a viewing stone (*suiseki*), or a figurine. Only one bonsai at a time should be used in a formal setting. Rotate specimens to highlight one that is flowering or just to change the display.

You may wish to set up a less formal display area with more space to display several specimens at once. It should be in a main room where you, your family, and friends spend a fair amount of time. In order to truly appreciate your herbal bonsai, they should be displayed where your eye can catch them at odd moments during the day. A landscaped herbal bonsai can be a meditative scene that allows your mind to rest as you are drawn within.

The most important consideration in setting up a display area is the viewing level. Bonsai are best appreciated when the center of the trunk is at eye level. Because it is easier for tall people to stoop down a little than it is for short people to stand on their toes, a display for standing viewers should be just a little on the low side. A display area set up in a sitting room should be at the appropriate height for people who are seated. Traditional displays in Japanese homes are low because people sit on pillows on the floor rather than on furniture. You may wish to place a bench or a couple of chairs in front of your display area so that viewers can be comfortable.

DECORATING THE DISPLAY AREA

There are many ways to decorate this display area and create the proper mood. Oriental decor is most appropriate and looks good in any home. Chopsticks and folding fans may be the first things that come to mind. Chinese paintings and hanging scrolls have traditionally been used for accenting bonsai display. Landscape paintings in particular help set the mood and complement the live plants. Woven mats of reeds or bamboo provide a natural appearance and can be hung on the wall, used as a curtain to close off the viewing area, or draped over a table or shelf. Use an oriental-looking calligraphy style for any labels or captions.

Folding screens (*shoji*), such as those used for movable walls in Japanese homes, also create an effective display area. It is best to use a solid color or natural wood to set off an area without drawing attention from the bonsai. There also are miniature *shoji* made of varnished wood and translucent paper that come as single or folding panels. Lamps made of the same materials are also available.

DISPLAY STANDS

Bonsai are traditionally displayed on a stand. For the best effect, match the stand to the style of the bonsai and the shape of the pot. A round pot should be placed on a round stand slightly larger in diameter than the pot. Massive, imposing bonsai with thick trunks need a solid stand with a thick table to balance the total appearance. Delicate, airy bonsai, such as many cascades, will look best on light stands with thin tables and skinny legs. A bonsai that leans strongly to the left or right should be placed to one side of a rectangular stand, allowing room to grow, or your herbal bonsai will seem to be leaping off the stand. A small companion plant can be used as an accent for such a bonsai to turn the empty expanse of varnished wood into a landscape and give depth to your setting.

There are many styles and shapes of tables and stands made out of solid wood using traditional and modern methods of Japanese joinery. Look for them at your local garden shop. If you can't find what you need in stock, they may be able to order it for you. These stands come in many shapes and sizes, including tall ones to use as floor stands or for displaying cascade bonsai, pedestal tops that fit onto posts, and even turntables that allow the viewer to rotate the bonsai and examine it from every angle.

You also can make your own bonsai stand or order something from a local woodworker. A slab of wood can be used as a simple stand if your bonsai doesn't doesn't need to be raised up off a shelf or table. Beautiful stands can be created out of slices cut from a log of an attractive hardwood, such as cherry, walnut, hickory, or oak. Sand the wood smooth and use a waterproof varnish or polyurethane sealer to protect it. Leave the bark intact, if possible. If the bark is damaged or looks bad, remove all of it and finish the edge as well. Beautiful slab bases also can be made from lumber that is cut to the appropriate shape and size. Use 2-inch thick lumber when making a base for a large bonsai in a big pot. A slab base should be just slightly larger than the pot. An inch or two of wood showing is about right.

COMPANION PLANTS

A shallow bonsai pot planted with a ground cover, dwarf bamboo (*Arundinaria pygmaea*), or a foliage plant can be placed in the display area as a companion plant to highlight your herbal bonsai and provide depth and mood to your setting. A grove of dwarf bamboo is a great accent plant that helps set the mood in an attractive display. The types of ground covers discussed in chapter 9 are those that best compliment an herbal bonsai. An herbal ground cover such as creeping thyme should be grown in a saucer or tray that is no more than 1 inch in height. When in full bloom, it will look like a field of wildflowers. You can grow a selection of ground covers for use as interchangeable accents to keep your display looking its best.

FOREST OR GROVE PLANTINGS

Forest or grove plantings are an interesting way to display herbal bonsai. You can combine several trees that are one-sided or less than ideal in shape to create a forest scene that has more impact than a single perfect bonsai. For the best results, use the same species for all the bonsai in the grove. This type of planting suggests a natural woodland scene, with rocks, ground covers, and bonsai of different size. You can plant a thick forest or scattered groves. The entire forest, and each small cluster or grove within that forest, should contain an odd number of trees to help create a random appearance similar to that of a natural forest.

Arrange the individual bonsai by viewing from directly above. Create a ground plan of irregular triangles for bonsai within a cluster and for the clusters within the entire grove. The largest tree should be planted one-third of the way in from the right or left edge and slightly toward the front of the landscape. The shortest trees should be planted near the rear to suggest depth and distance. The shape of the forest crown should also appear as a group of irregular triangles within the overall irregular triangle shape of the grove's crown. When viewed from the front or sides, no single bonsai should be directly in front of another. Although most groves are wilderness scenes, you may add figurines or other decorations to suit your taste. As groves become larger and more complicated, they become miniature landscapes.

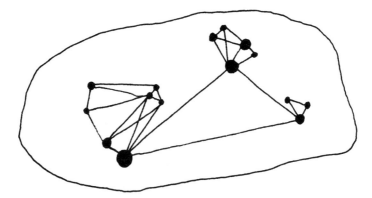

An overhead ground plan is useful when creating groves.

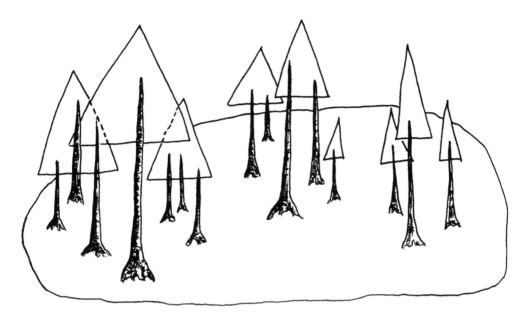

Larger trees in the front and smaller trees in the back will give an illusion of distance. A front-view ground plan is helpful in this case.

MINIATURE LANDSCAPES

Saikei is a Japanese style wherein the planting resembles a larger landscape area than the typical grove. Rocks are used to represent cliffs or mountains, and water is used in shallow pools or is suggested by white sand. Smaller bonsai are used in miniature landscapes than would be used in most grove plantings. Microenvironments as developed by Dr. Leon Snyder, professor of horticulture at the University of Missouri–Columbia, are large, 3-to 5-foot landscapes that are planned as accurate representations of natural scenes. Forces of nature, such as wind, erosion, and other geological aspects, are considered and shown. Different species of bonsai are often used in separate groves within the landscape. Some of these microenvironments include streams and waterfalls, with running water powered by hidden electric pumps.

Chinese rock planting (*pen-jing*) and Japanese viewing stones (*suiseki*) are related art forms that are often displayed with bonsai. *Pen-jing* consists of natural rocks arranged on a slab of marble or a large, very shallow tray to resemble an intricate landscape. These rocks are often surrounded with sand, soil, or water. Much care is taken in choosing and arranging the rocks, and many named landscape styles have been developed through history. These rock plantings may be left spare and simple or may be decorated with small bonsai, ground covers, and possibly figurines.

Suiseki consists of a single stone often used to suggest a specific natural feature, such as a mountain, island, lake, waterfall, or plateau. It can also be just a beautiful rock that resembles nothing but is appreciated for its beauty. Suiseki are displayed on slabs or shallow trays filled with sand or gravel. Occasionally it will be surrounded by moss. Figurines or larger plants are never used. The most attractive stands are cut and polished wood that is carved to match the exact shape of the bottom of the viewing stone.

Both of these rock planting styles look extremely good when displayed with bonsai, and they are fascinating arts worth pursuing in their own right. The ultimate in *pen-jing* or *suiseki* is to collect rock from a particular place and then use that rock to create a visual representation of the landscape at that location. Just one rock planting will do a lot to enhance any group of herbal bonsai.

This microenvironment created by Dr. Leon Snyder is his representation of the Needle's Eye, a formation along the Buffalo River in Arkansas.

AFTERWORD

MY BONSAI TEACHER, Leon Snyder, professor of horticulture at the University of Missouri–Columbia, once taught a week-long seminar to fifty members of the American Bonsai Society and their guests, who included several Japanese bonsai masters. Dr. Snyder's specialty and the topic of this class was microenvironmental design. This consists of combining bonsai, rocks, and ground covers in a landscape planting that often has a running stream (maintained with a pump) integral to the overall design. On one particular landscape of elm groves with a babbling brook, Dr. Snyder had used a special leaf-dwarfing technique. After plucking the first set of leaves produced in the spring (a common practice on traditional deciduous bonsai), he sprayed the new, emerging leaves with dwarfing hormones used commonly in the bedding plant industry. This reduced the elm's normal 1-inch leaves to beautiful dark green miniatures only $^1/_4$ inch long. His bonsai was a spectacular display of scale with such tiny leaves.

I came upon a Japanese bonsai master sitting in a chair he had moved right in front of this elm grove landscape. I walked up to greet him, but this man was leaning forward, gazing intensely into the landscape. Tears were flowing freely down his cheeks and dripping off his chin. I was profoundly moved and couldn't disturb his concentration. This was one of those transcendental experiences that still gives me chills as I write about it twenty years later. That moment changed my life. Seeing the depths of this man's reaction to a piece of art was a profoundly spiritual experience that deepened my appreciation of bonsai to a religious intensity.

From its origins, bonsai has been associated with religious and philosophical traditions. Bonsai were grown in ancient Buddhist monasteries during the Chin dynasty, and the earliest paintings showing bonsai were pictures of scholars and the nobility. Some of the early bonsai masters that gained fame in China were monks. This association continued because there are deep philosophical underpinnings to the art of bonsai. At a transcendental level, the soul of the artist joins with the spirit of the tree in a mutual expression of artistic intent. Without the plant, the artist has only a vision in his imagination. Without the artist, the bonsai tree is merely a potted plant. When the two come together in creating what is actually an illusionary representation of nature, both artist and viewer partake of the spiritual side of bonsai.

REFERENCES AND RESOURCES

BOOKS

Barton, Dan. *The Bonsai Book.* London: Ebury Press, 1990.

Behme, Robert Lee. *Bonsai, Saikei and Bonkei: Japanese Dwarf Trees and Tray Landscapes.* New York: William Morrow and Company, Inc., 1969.

Bollmann, Willi E. *Kamuti: A New Way in Bonsai.* London: Faber and Faber Limited, 1974.

Chan, Peter. *Create Your Own Bonsai with Everyday Garden Plants.* Vancouver: Cavendish Books, 1991.

Clifford, Patricia Hart, ed. *Bonsai: Culture and Care of Miniature Trees.* 2nd ed. Menlo Park, CA: Lane Publishing Co., 1977.

Gustafson, Herb L. *The Bonsai Workshop.* New York: Sterling Publishing Company, 1994.

Kawasumi, Masakuni. *Bonsai with American Trees.* Tokyo: Kodansha International Ltd., 1975.

Lesniewicz, Paul. *Bonsai in Your Home.* New York: Sterling Publishing Company, 1994.

——. *Bonsai: The Complete Guide to Art and Technique.* Dorset: Blandford Press, 1984.

Liang, Amy. *The Living Art of Bonsai.* New York: Sterling Publishing Company, 1992.

McDowell, Jack, ed. *Bonsai: Culture and Care of Miniature Trees.* Menlo Park, CA: Lane Books, 1974.

Walker, Linda. *Bonsai.* New York: Drake Publishers, 1972.

Woollard, Leslie. *Japanese and Miniature Gardens.* Yorkshire: Litton, Magna Print Books, 1974.

SOURCES OF INFORMATION

American Bonsai Society
P.O. Box 95
Bedford, NY 10506

Bonsai Clubs International
2354 Lida Drive
Mountain View, CA 94040

Brooklyn Botanic Garden
1000 Washington Avenue
Brooklyn, NY 11225

MAIL-ORDER NURSERIES

Logee's Greenhouses, Ltd.
141 North Street
Danielson, CT 06239-1939

Nichols Garden Nursery
1198 Pacific
Albany, OR 97321

The Sandy Mush Herb Nursery
316 Surrett Cove Road
Leicester, NC 28748-9622